JAGUAR CARS LTD.
COVENTRY

THE C-TYPE REGISTER

Compiler **Terry Larson**

Editors Penny Graham and
Anders Ditlev Clausager

Publisher

This Register is published by the Jaguar Daimler Heritage Trust in England, and the Classic Jaguar Association, Inc., based on information supplied by owners of the cars.

Notice

Chassis numbers and other identifying information listed in this register are provided by the car owners and several other sources. This is opinion only and not necessarily fact. Owners and prospective owners are advised to investigate the histories of the cars and chassis numbers. Neither the Jaguar Daimler Heritage Trust, Jaguar Cars Limited, its employees and associates, nor the Classic Jaguar Association and its Registrar Terry Larson, will warrant the authenticity or accuracy of information. Whilst every care has been taken to record accurately the information given to us by owners, the publisher will not be held responsible for any omissions, errors, or the consequences thereof.

First Edition, 1999-2001

Designed, produced and printed by Warwicks UK Limited, Coventry, England

Cover illustration by the late Richard Corson, courtesy Jaguar Journal magazine.

The Jaguar Daimler Heritage Trust

The JDHT was established as a charitable educational trust in 1983 with the support of Jaguar Cars Limited, to preserve for the benefit of the nation a collection of motor vehicles manufactured by Jaguar and associated companies, together with a collection of artefacts and records relating to these companies and their products. The JDHT is housed in a purpose-built museum, opened in 1998, in the spiritual home of Jaguar, the historic factory in Browns Lane, Coventry, England. The museum is open to the public, and a selection of vehicles from the JDHT collection is always on display. Please contact us for further information on the JDHT and the services we offer to the public.

Jaguar Daimler Heritage Trust, Jaguar Cars Limited, Browns Lane, Allesley, Coventry CV5 9DR, England
Telephone +44 (0)24 7640 2121, facsimile +44 (0)24 7640 5581

Classic Jaguar Association, Inc.

The Classic Jaguar Association, Inc. is a non-profit international club dedicated to the preservation and enjoyment of SS and older Jaguar cars. The Association concentrates on publication of a fine newsletter called, News & Technical Bulletin, together with publication of several Registers for various models of SS and older Jaguar cars. There are club activities in parts of the USA where membership is large enough to support such activities. For information about the Club, or to submit corrections or additions to the Register Listings, please write to the Registrar:

Terry Larson, 2929 N. 82nd St, Mesa, Arizona 85207, USA
Telephone: +1 480-984-8501, facsimile: +1 480-984-5219
E-Mail tlljaguar@cs.com
Classic Jaguar Association registrar of C-types, D-types, and Lightweight E-types

Frank Billeter *Photo courtesy Billeter family*

Dedication: Frank Billeter

This Register is dedicated to the memory of the late Frank H Billeter, who was the Membership Director for the Jaguar Club of Central Arizona. Frank kindly offered to do the computer work but sadly passed away before he was able to finish.
A special thank you goes to his wife Sharon and their son Eric, who stepped in and completed the project.

Stirling Moss in XKC 002 winning the 1951 TT race. *Photo ©JDHT*

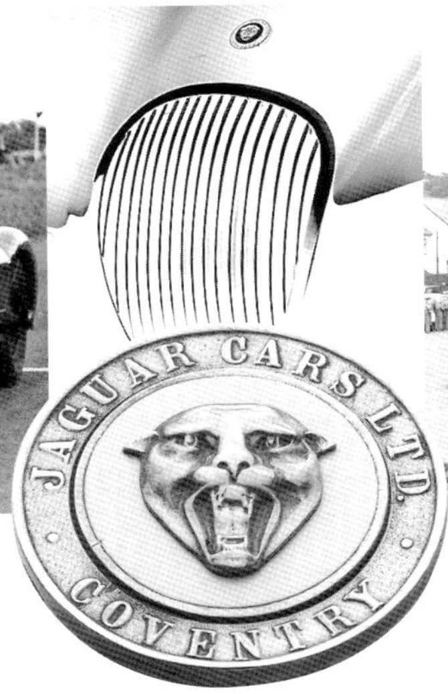

The C-types return to the Jaguar factory at Browns Lane after the 1953 Le Mans *Photo Unwin/JDHT*

C-TIME IS FOUR O'CLOCK

What possessed Jaguar to do it? Was it a kind of corporate hubris? How on earth did William Lyons and Bill Heynes imagine that they could build a completely new car within a space of a few months, take the untried car to the most famous and most difficult motor race in the world, and stand any chance of winning?

But they did, didn't they. Nothing much more needs to be said. *And yet:*

Jaguar was still a young company. Barely twenty years had elapsed since the first SS1 had been manufactured. Some experience had been gained in competition, but Jaguar was still a newcomer in this field. Now, in the brave new post-war world, the goal posts had moved. For Jaguar, and for the British motor industry in general, the focus had shifted. It was no longer sufficient to build small numbers of cars for a well-defined clientele in the home market. Spurred by the government's 'export or die' policy, it was now necessary to bring the marque of Jaguar to the attention of a new, worldwide audience.

The ambition of the founder, William Lyons, was to make a high-performance luxury saloon, which would set the standard in the international market. Therefore, a new engine of almost revolutionary specification for a mass production car was put in hand already during the war. Previously, only small manufacturers with a racing background (Bugatti, Alfa Romeo) had built engines with two overhead camshafts. Now, Jaguar planned to conquer the world with such a design.

To allow for any teething troubles to be cured fairly painlessly, at first the XK engine was introduced in what was planned as a limited production sports car, the XK120 unveiled at the first post-war London Motor Show in 1948. Demand for this stunningly beautiful car was such that Jaguar had to change their plans and put a modified version into large-scale production. The new model proved to have such a performance that it soon became a natural choice for motor sport. As well as many private owners, the Jaguar company also decided to enter motor racing with the XK120.

And so in 1950, a works supported team of three XK120s appeared in the 24-hour race at Le Mans in France. Le Mans was a natural choice. Since its inception in 1923, it had quickly gained recognition as the premier race for touring cars. It unique format – twenty-four hours of continuous racing, from 4pm to 4pm through the short June night – had been devised as the ultimate test of endurance and reliability. Entrants originally had to be production cars of 'touring' type, although regulations were later relaxed to allow the entry also of prototypes.

Not only did Le Mans have a very special place in the hearts of British enthusiasts who remembered the singular record of five victories by the Bentleys in the 1920s, but it was also recognised as the most important international motor race. In an era when Formula 1 Grand Prix races tended to be exclusively Italian contests, Le Mans attracted a truly international field, from the USA to Czechoslovakia, as well as some weird and wonderful entrants. Any car that won at Le Mans was certain to achieve international fame.

At Le Mans in 1950, the three works supported XK120s performed very creditably. Indeed, one Jaguar held on to third place until the clutch expired with three hours to go, and the two surviving cars finished twelfth and fifteenth. Bearing in mind that the winner was an only lightly camouflaged Grand Prix car with a 4.5-litre engine against the near-standard 3.4-litre Jaguar, the result could only be described as encouraging.

Jaguar's chief engineer, Bill Heynes, did a few calculations and decided that it might actually be possible to win Le Mans with a lighter, more powerful and more aerodynamic car. His boss, William Lyons (who was as always mindful of expenditure) was eventually persuaded to give his consent to a programme which involved the design of such a car, and the entry at Le Mans and in other selected races.

And so to 1951. It was a different world then. One sailed across the Atlantic by Cunard liner, rather than flying by Jumbo. Most people did not go abroad at all, and motoring on the other side of the Channel was still considered something of an adventure. Nylon stockings and ballpoint pens were distinct novelties, and instead of watching the single channel on TV, most people listened to the Home Service. There was a brand-new daily radio programme called 'The Archers'.

Start of the 1951 Le Mans, with the privately-entered XK120 amongst the three team cars *Photo Pruvost/JDHT*

The Labour government of Clement Attlee would be toppled in that autumn's election, which brought back Churchill as Prime Minister. Britain was actually at war in Korea, and was also becoming increasingly embroiled in the 'Cold War'. Britain still had an Empire, although a shrinking one, and it was now called the Commonwealth. Some rationing was still in force, while space flight and computers were the staples of science fiction writing. However, to demonstrate that war was truly behind us and the nation was confident about the future, the Festival of Britain was a powerful symbol and a popular attraction.

That Jaguar had a potential ace up their sleeve was first revealed to a wider public when a description and a photo were published in The Motor for 20 June 1951 of the new XK120C – 'C' for competition – followed two days later by more details in The Autocar. This was in the week before the 24-hour race at Le Mans, where, as announced in the magazines, Jaguar planned to run a team of three of these cars. A top speed of 150mph was predicted. As stated in The Autocar,

'The Type C (sic) was put in hand about eight months ago, and therefore there has not been too much time to bring the cars up to the pitch of their perfection. But everyone will wish them success in their maiden race.'

which in retrospect was a brilliant understatement. Only a week later the two journals were ecstatic to report the complete and crushing victory of the new Jaguar, driven by Peter Walker and Peter Whitehead, at a new record for average speed and distance, and having led the race for sixteen out of twenty-four hours. In addition, Stirling Moss in one of the other C-types had set a new record for the fastest lap before his car retired. Despite two of the three C-types retiring with loss of oil pressure, the winning car proved that the C-type basically had not only the speed but also the reliability to win this most demanding of all motor races. Indeed, on Sunday 24 June 1951, four o'clock was C-time.

Because the C-type was such a single-race car, and because Jaguar had fixed its sights on Le Mans victory, the record of the model in other races was always a bit patchy. No C-type finished the Mille Miglia, or achieved a good placing in the Targa Florio. However, C-types did come first and second in the 1951 Tourist Trophy race, and won the 1953 12-hour race at Reims.

THE AMBITION OF THE FOUNDER, WILLIAM LYONS, WAS TO MAKE A HIGH-PERFORMANCE LUXURY SALOON, WHICH WOULD SET THE STANDARD IN THE INTERNATIONAL MARKET.

In 1952, Jaguar – or perhaps their aerodynamicist Malcolm Sayer – tried to be too clever. The bodywork on the works C-types was modified in an effort to lower drag, and this was a contributory reason why all three Le Mans cars overheated and retired. The gradual elimination of the Ferraris, Gordinis and Talbots brought eventual victory to another newcomer, the Mercedes-Benz 300SL of Germany. Any hubris on the part of Jaguar was effectively checked.

A lesson learned, in 1953 the works Jaguars turned up at Le Mans looking just like the 1951 cars, although there were plenty of improvements under the skin – the cars were lighter, the rear suspension was improved, while the engines were fitted with Weber carburettors and had usefully more power. The secret weapon, however, was the new disc brake developed jointly with Dunlop. This gave the Jaguars an important advantage, even against the much more powerful Cunninghams and Ferraris. The result was immensely gratifying. The three works Jaguars finished first, second and fourth, and a privately entered production C-type was ninth. The winning car for the first time in Le Mans history averaged more than 100mph, at 105.841mph an improvement of almost ten per cent over the previous record.

Malcolm Sayer's wooden model of the C-type
Photo ©JDHT

George Weaver in XKC 009 (front ca
and Phil Hill in XKC 007 (behind) a
technical inspection, Elkhart Lake,
September 1952
Photo courtesy Godfrey Miller

Phil Hill in XKC 007, Elkhart Lake,
September 1952
Photo courtesy Gerald Nell

Victory parade at Coventry Council House after the 1953 Le Mans
Photo Daily Mirror/JDHT

That Jaguar and Britain should win this important race in the year of the Coronation of Her Majesty Queen Elizabeth II gave a particular poignancy to the event. According to The Motor for 24 June 1953, following their victory the Jaguar team despatched a telegram to the secretary of HM The Queen:

'The Jaguar team humbly present their loyal duty to Her Majesty and advise her that in her Coronation year they have won for Britain the world's greatest international car race at Le Mans, France, yesterday. Signed: Jaguar, Coventry.'

And were rewarded with the following reply:

'The Queen was very pleased to learn of the success of the Jaguar team. Please convey Her Majesty's sincere thanks to all members of it for their kind and loyal message. Signed: Private Secretary to the Queen, Buckingham Palace.'

In the longer term, perhaps, the victory of Le Mans and the 'loyal message' may have played a part in William Lyons receiving the accolade of a knighthood in the 1956 New Year's Honours List, the visit shortly afterwards by the Queen and Prince Philip to the Jaguar factory, and more and more members of the Royal family – including Her Majesty – choosing Jaguars for personal transport. After the 1953 season, however, the C-type soon faded from first line events, so quickly did developments occur in motor racing in those years. Jaguar had another new car coming along, the D-type which would eventually score three Le Mans victories. The works C-types were scrapped or sold, but the production cars sold to private owners often continued to race in a great variety of events on both sides of the Atlantic Ocean.

Indeed, so it continues to this day. The staying power and continued successes of the C-types, virtually all of which survive, are documented in scholarly detail by Terry Larson in the individual car histories that make up the greater part of this book. I am delighted that the Jaguar Daimler Heritage Trust, and in particular Penny Graham, herself a C-type owner and campaigner, have been able to play a part in the publication of this compendium. While it may strike the casual browser as an accumulation of facts, it is a valuable contribution to Jaguar history. To document the car histories in such detail is also a guard against the mix-up of car identities, to which Terry alludes in his introduction.

As a contrast, perhaps, to the factual style of the individual car histories, let me finish this part of the story with a quote from the novel The Last Open Road by Burt Levy, first published by Think Fast Ink of Oak Park, Illinois, USA in 1994. A bit of scene setting: It is 1952, and our young hero Buddy Palumbo, a New Jersey grease monkey, has graduated from tuning MG TCs to working on a wealthy client's XK120, when he is suddenly thrust into the world of serious racing, through the good offices of Colin St John and Barry Spline of the not entirely fictional Westbridge Motor Car Company, Ltd. Buddy is asked to ferry one of two brand-new C-types from Manhattan to Elkhart Lake, Wisconsin, for their debut race in the USA (the intelligent reader will realise that these cars were XKC 007 and XKC 009!). Here, then, is Buddy's description of his first encounter with the C-types:

'But before anybody could say another word, we came up over the top of the ramp and right directly in front of us, lit up in our headlights, were two low, sleek, liquid-smooth puddles of aluminum alloy with short, graceful racing windscreens and knockoff wire wheels. One was painted a green so deep and dark it was almost black, and the other was a soft, gleaming silver-grey, and you could tell right off they were

Dashboard of XKC 009, tak
during technical inspectio
Elkhart Lake, September 1
Photo courtesy Tom Groskritz

IT IS 1952, AND OUR YOUNG HERO BUDDY PALUMBO, A NEW JERSEY GREASE MONKEY, HAS GRADUATED FROM TUNING MG TCS TO WORKING ON A WEALTHY CLIENT'S XK120, WHEN HE IS SUDDENLY THRUST INTO THE WORLD OF SERIOUS RACING.

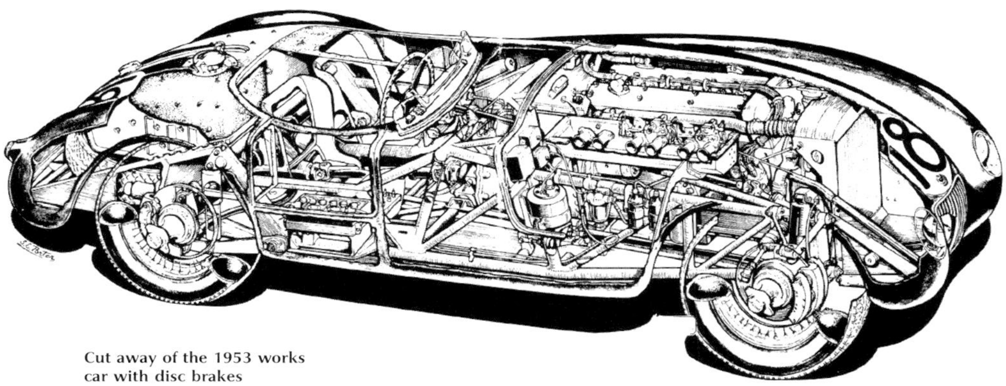

Cut away of the 1953 works car with disc brakes
Photo The Motor/JDHT

Jaguars, on account of the rounded, upright grilles with thin, curved vertical bars and the bronze cat's-head medallions just above them. But right there any resemblance between those two cars and any Jaguar automobile I'd ever seen came to a sudden, startling halt. Why, those two were racing cars – no two ways about it! – single-minded, pure-blooded, and purpose-built to be lower and tighter to the ground than any road-going Jag 120 you ever saw. They were both righthand drive (what else?) and had riveted woodrim steering wheels and sleek, faired-in plexiglass covers over the headlamps to try and cheat the wind at high speed. A pair of naked exhaust pipes ran along the rocker panels on the passenger side, and the mufflers didn't amount to much more than a couple empty tin cans stuck on as an afterthought. Like you were really going to drive something like this on the damn highway, right? "Jee-zus, Barry," I gasped, "what the hell are those things?"

By now, you should be able to answer that simple question easily enough. Please read for yourself the chapters where Buddy describes the drive to Wisconsin in convoy with racing driver Tommy Edwards, and the actual race where Phil Hill (non-fictional) in the silver C-type beats Tommy (for whom Buddy, as his mechanic, is naturally rooting) in the green car. It is a wonderfully evocative description of an era when motor racing still offered glamour, excitement – and thrills – in a way that we can barely imagine, fifty years later, as we watch to-day's Grand Prix processions on our television screens.

Then again, you could always make a point of going to watch C-types and others of their ilk in action at a historic race meeting!

Anders Ditlev Clausager
Coventry, May 2001

William Lyons and David Brown (of Aston Martin) discuss their chances before the 1951 Le Mans
Photo Klementaski/JDHT

Phil Hill at speed in XKC 007, Elkhart Lake, September 1952
Photo courtesy Gerald Nell

Foreword by Terry Larson

After seeing the racing success of the standard XK120 in 1950, William Lyons gave Bill Heynes the go-ahead to design and build a lighter, more aerodynamic car using standard XK 120 mechanicals. The car was built for a single purpose, to win at Le Mans. The car was named the XK120C or C-type - C for competition.

The first three Le Mans C-types were hand built in only six weeks. They were then entered by the factory in the 1951 Le Mans race. While two retired and did not finish the race, XKC 003 driven by Peter Whitehead and Peter Walker won and came in 77 miles ahead of the second placed car. Additionally, they established the following new records:

Fastest lap speed: 105.232 mph
New 24 hour speed record: 93.495 mph
Greatest distance travelled in the 24 hours: 2,243.886 miles

The Whitehead/Walker car, XKC 003, soon after the start of the 1951 Le Mans, followed by the Cunninghams
Photo ©JDHT

An impressive showing for the first time out, this was just the beginning of a period of domination at Le Mans for the Jaguar factory. A domination like few other marques have accomplished before or since.

The information contained in this register comes from several years of research gathered from many sources. Special thanks are due to the many who helped in the information gathering process: Frank, Sharon and Eric Billeter, Tom Candlish, Colin Cook, Norman Dewis, Steve Earle, the late Lofty England, Aubrey Finburgh, Penny Graham, Tom Groskritz, Holly Hollenbeck, Jaguar Cars Limited, Jaguar Daimler Heritage Trust, Peter Jaye, Chris Keith-Lucas, Burt Levy, Terry McGrath, John Maries, Godfrey Miller, John Pearson, Philip Porter, Paul Skilleter (Jaguar World magazine), Ole Sommer, Jim Unsworth, Charles Vacy-Ash, the late Andrew Whyte, as well as many others. We are particularly grateful to the many C-type owners who provided personal reminiscences and photographs in addition to the basic histories of their cars.

This Register will be updated periodically. Period photos used are from my archives, or the JDHT. Photos supplied from other sources, including many private owners, have been credited individually where they appear. I hope you find this information interesting. Any additional photos (period or current), suggestions or bona fide information that could be supplied for future registers would be most welcome.

Owners of C-types were asked to contribute histories and information of their individual cars according to the following standards: The requirement for listing in these pages is that the machine involved must have an original chassis or an early factory replacement chassis and continuous history. This arbitrary requirement might mean that some cars which are substantially composed of original parts such as body, etc. might not be listed while a car carrying nothing original but the chassis, would be listed. Such a system would seem to be necessary to prevent the eventual listing of more cars than were originally made. Unbroken and Continuous History means simply that the car involved has been a known car throughout its life with a complete chain of ownership. This is very important.

There are cases in which the body went one way, the chassis another, and the result is two cars! In these cases the car bearing the body only (or even the body and some drive train components) will not be listed – although it could be argued that such a car has more original pieces than another, which is listed. The chassis-only rule precludes arguments about listing machines with 'many original parts,' etc.

Concerning reproductions: Reproduction cars, often called replicas, are known to exist in fair numbers. That such cars would be built up is to be expected since the value of the genuine cars is now such that reproduction would perhaps be the only way an enthusiast might own such a car. While a reproduction car might be an acceptable alternative for such an enthusiast, still it is hoped that those who sell (or re-sell) these cars do not lose sight of the fact that they are indeed reproduction cars. It is probably reasonable to say that the time when a reproduction becomes a counterfeit is the time when the chassis number from a missing, destroyed, or genuine car is affixed.

Please also refer to the section 'Glossary of terms' in the appendix on page 76

Terry Larson, Mesa, Arizona, USA

Abbreviations

ARDC	Australian Racing Drivers' Club
ASRA	American Sports Racing Association (?)
BSCOA	British Sports Car Club of America
BRSCC	British Racing and Sports Car Club
FIR	Firebird International Raceway, Phoenix,Arizona
JCNA	Jaguar Clubs of North America
HMSA	Historic Motor Sports Association, USA (?)
LISCA	Long Island Sports Car Association
NHIS	New Hampshire International Speedway
PIR	Phoenix International Raceway, Phoenix,Arizona
RCA	Racing Club of America (?)
SCCA	Sports Car Club of America
USCCA	United Sports Car Clubs of America
VARA	Vintage Auto Racing Association, USA
VSCA	Vintage Sports Car Club of America

SPECIFICATIONS AND GENERAL INFORMATION

Engine

Block – Made from cast iron chrome alloy, six cylinders with a bore of 83mm and a stroke of 106 mm, which give it a displacement of 3442cc. The flat top Brico aluminium solid skirt pistons are fitted to EN.16 manganese molybdenum steel connecting rods. The EN-16 counterweighted crankshaft is carried in seven $2^3/_4$ inch steel-backed white metal (lead-indium bronze) bearings. Pistons were available in 8, 8.5 and 9:1 compression ratios. The steel flywheel was lightened and the damper made of steel. Engine block casting number C4820 will be found on the upper right-hand side. The engine number should be stamped above the oil filter. Not all blocks were so stamped however. A full flow Tecalemit oil filter is fitted. Some early sumps were made of steel while others were cast in two pieces of aluminium bolted together horizontally, with wings on the lower side for added capacity.

Head - The head is aluminium alloy with hemispheric combustion chambers, valves in V formation and two overhead camshafts. The camshafts are driven by a two-stage duplex roller chain with hydraulic tensioning. The overhead valves are inclined at seventy degrees. The camshaft lift is $^3/_8$ inch. Valve springs, which will not bounce below 6500rpm, are selected and fitted. The valve seats are Austenitic steel. The port sizes are 1 $^3/_8$ inch for inlet and 1 $^1/_4$ inch for exhaust. Carburation was initially by twin 1 $^3/_4$ inch S.U.'s, later twin 2 inch S.U.'s, and finally three Webers. Standard cast twin exhaust manifolds are used. Some factory cars have welded-up manifolds, Chassis numbers 051, 052, and 053 use manifolds made of 20 gauge 'inconol' tubes. With a compression ratio of 8:1 and using 80 octane fuel, the engine produces 200bhp at 5,800 rpm. Engines fitted with 40mm Webers develop 218.5bhp, at 5250rpm

Transmission

The gearbox is a Jaguar built close ratio unit, similar to the version available as an option on the XK 120. The clutch is a Borg and Beck dry single plate clutch with solid centre and bonded riveted lining. The 'lightweight' cars (051, 052, and 053) are fitted with a constant mesh first gear and a triple plate Borg and Beck clutch. The rear axle is a standard Salisbury XK120 unit, with added welded on brackets for the special suspension. Several alternative ratios were available and late factory cars have limited slip differentials.

Chassis

The chassis is constructed from a combination of channel section members and tubes. The suspension is independent at the front with wishbones and torsion bar springs. The specially controlled rear axle has transverse torsion bar springs and torque reaction couplings, on later cars also a Panhard rod. Newton hydraulic dampers are used front and rear. The brakes were originally the same as on the standard XK120, 12 inch Lockheed drum brakes with tandem hydraulic master cylinders, and ratchet type automatic adjustment on the front brakes. The 'lightweight' cars had very special Dunlop disc brakes, with multi pad calipers and chromed steel discs. (Experimental disc brakes were used on 005 and 011 by the factory, but were removed before these cars were sold.) The wheels are Dunlop 16 inch centre lock wire wheels, with 54 spokes in two rows and aluminium rims. The tyres are Dunlop 6.50x16 road racing. The fuel system uses a 40 gallon rear mounted tank (flexible tank on 1953 works cars) and has two S.U. electric pumps.

Main dimensions

Wheelbase	8ft 0in	2438mm
Track	4ft 3in	1295mm
Overall length	13ft 1in	3988mm
Width	5ft 4in	1638mm
Height	3ft 2in	978mm
Ground clearance	5in	140mm
Turning circle	31in	9.45m
Dry weight, approx.	18.5cwt	
	(2072lb)	941kg

Identification

The chassis, body, engine and gearbox numbers are found collectively on a plate fixed to the bulkhead in the engine bay. If the chassis plate is genuine and the car retains its original components, the numbers should correspond with those stamped on the individual components as follows:

Chassis: Stamped on the right upper shock absorber tower and sometimes directly behind the radiator.
Engine: Stamped on the block above the oil filter housing (not all cars had the numbers stamped), and also at the front of the valley of the cylinder head. The flywheel will have the engine number stamped as well.
Gearbox: Stamped on the raised boss at the upper left rear of the casing and on the top cover.
Body: Stamped on the body tag near or under the chassis plate, on the underside of the bonnet on the exhaust side, and between the seat backs.

Note: Not all cars had chassis plates.

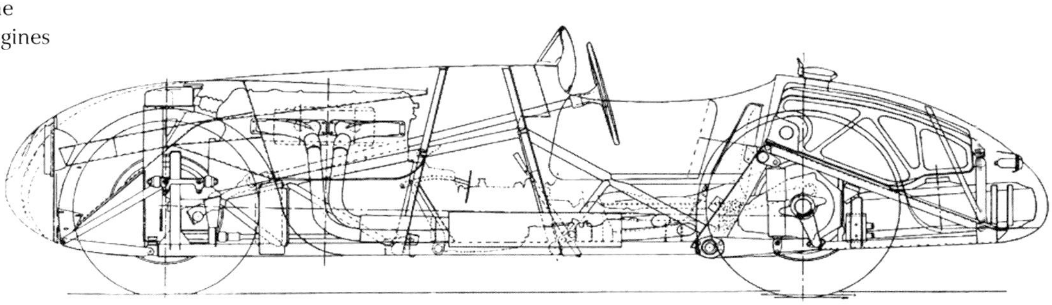

Line drawing of the general arrangment of the C-type
Photo ©JDHT

THE C-TYPE JAGUARS: SUMMARY

The works cars

XKC 001, XKC 002, XKC 003, XKC 008, XKC 011, XKC 012, XKC037, XKC 047, XKC 051, XKC 052, XKC 053, XKC 054 (the C/D prototype).

The Le Mans cars

Year	Chassis no	Entrant	Drivers	Result	Retirement
1951	XKC 003	drivers	Whitehead/Walker	first	
1951	XKC 002	drivers	Moss/Fairman	did not finish	retired, con rod broke
1951	XKC 001	drivers	Johnson/Biondetti	did not finish	retired, loss of oil pressure
1952	XKC 001	works	Rolt/Hamilton	did not finish	fourth hour, blown gasket
1952	XKC 011	P D C Walker	Moss/Walker	did not finish	third hour, engine
1952	XKC 002	works	Whitehead/Stewart	did not finish	first hour, blown gasket
1953	XKC 051	works	Rolt/Hamilton	first	
1953	XKC 053	works	Moss/Walker	second	
1953	XKC 052	works	Whitehead/Stewart	fourth	
1953	XKC 047	Ecurie Francorchamps	Laurent/de Tornaco	ninth	
1954	XKC 047	Ecurie Francorchamps	Laurent/Swaters	fourth	

The Mille Miglia cars

Year	Chassis no	Drivers	Result
1952	XKC 003	Moss/Dewis	retired
1953	XKC 005	Rolt/Hayden	retired
1953	XKC 008	Johnson/?	retired
1953	XKC 011	Moss/Goodall	retired
1953	XKC 016	Descollanges/Ugnon	crashed
1953	XKC 035	Heaurtaux/ Mme.Heaurtaux	not classified
1953	XKC 045	Tadini/Cortese	retired

The Targa Florio cars

Year	Chassis no	Drivers	Result
1953	XKC 011	Wisdom	seventeenth
1956	XKC 038	Margulies/Piper	sixteenth

The Reims cars

Year	Race	Chassis no	Drivers	Result
1952	50 laps, 225 miles	XKC 005	Moss	first
1953	12-hour	XKC 012	Whitehead/Moss	first
1953	12-hour	XKC 046	Sanderson/Douglas	fourth
1954	12-hour	XKC 037	Manussis/Dunham	retired
1954	12-hour	XKC 047	Laurent/Swaters	third

The Tourist Trophy cars

Year	Chassis no	Drivers	Result
1951	XKC 001	Johnson/Rolt	fourth
1951	XKC 002	Moss	first
1951	XKC 003	Walker	second
1953	XKC 012	Whitehead/Stewart	did not finish
1953	XKC 050	Fairman	seventh
1953	XKC 051	Rolt/Hamilton	did not finish
1953	XKC 053	Moss/Walker	did not finish
1954	XKC 050	Flynn/Large	thirteenth

THE ECURIE ECOSSE CARS

XKC 006, XKC 041, XKC 042, XKC 046

LIST IN CHASSIS NUMBER ORDER, WITH CURRENT REGISTRATION MARKS

XKC 004	MDU 214
XKC 005	MDU 212
XKC 006	JWS 353
XKC 008	MHP 825
XKC 011	POV 114
XKC 013	VSU 669
XKC 014	VSU 268
XKC 015	TKV 500
XKC 019	UFF 376
XKC 021	PUG 676
XKC 024	878 FUF
XKC 025	XSV 894
XKC 027	OS
XKC 029	JSV 258
XKC 035	WWK 4
XKC 036	OLT 393
XKC 037	NDU 970
XKC 038	OVC 915
XKC 039	RKX 991
XKC 040	SEH 721
XKC 041	KSF 181
XKC 042	KSF 182
XKC 043	PUR 120
XKC 045	NDU 289
XKC 046	MVC 630
XKC 048	OHP 43
XKC 049	RAU 450
XKC 050	SVM 737
XKC 051	LSF 420
XKC 052	LSF 672
XKC 053	WKA 9

The man from Dunlop checks the tyres, before the start of the 1951 Ulster Tourist Trophy, Dundrod
Photo ©JDHT

LIST IN ORDER OF CURRENT REGISTRATION MARKS, WITH CHASSIS NUMBERS

878 FUF	XKC 024
JSV 258	XKC 029
JWS 353	XKC 006
KSF 181	XKC 041
KSF 182	XKC 042
LSF 420	XKC 051
LSF 672	XKC 052
MDU 212	XKC 005
MDU 214	XKC 004
MHP 825	XKC 008
MVC 630	XKC 046
NDU 289	XKC 045
NDU 970	XKC 037
OHP 43	XKC 048
OLT 393	XKC 036
OS	XKC 027
OVC 915	XKC 038
POV 114	XKC 011
PUG 676	XKC 021
PUR 120	XKC 043
RAU 450	XKC 049
RKX 991	XKC 039
SEH 721	XKC 040
SVM 737	XKC 050
TKV 500	XKC 015
UFF 376	XKC 019
VSU 669	XKC 013
WKA 9	XKC 053
WWK 4	XKC 035
VSU 268	XKC 014
XSV 894	XKC 025

PRODUCTION CARS, DELIVERIES WHEN NEW, LISTED BY COUNTRY

USA:	XKC 007, XKC 009, XKC 010, XKC 013, XKC 014, XKC 015, XKC 017, XKC 020, XKC 022, XKC 023, XKC 024, XKC 026, XKC 028, XKC 029, XKC 030, XKC 031, XKC 033, XKC 034
United Kingdom:	XKC 004, XKC 005, XKC 006, XKC 008, XKC 021, XKC 039, XKC 040, XKC 041, XKC 042, XKC 048, XKC 049
Belgium:	XKC 018, XKC 019, XKC 032, XKC 047
France:	XKC 016, XKC 035, XKC 046
Morocco:	XKC 025, XKC 036
Holland:	XKC 043
Ireland:	XKC 050
Italy:	XKC 045
Sweden:	XKC 044
Switzerland:	XKC 027

Note: 42% of all new production C-types were sent to the USA

PRODUCTION CARS, AS CURRENTLY OWNED, LISTED BY COUNTRY

USA:	XKC 007, XKC 009, XKC 010, XKC 012, XKC 014, XKC 017, XKC 018, XKC 022, XKC 024, XKC 026, XKC 028, XKC 030, XKC 031, XKC 032, XKC 033, XKC 034, XKC 036, XKC 037, XKC 040, XKC 044, XKC 046, XKC 049, XKC 050, XKC 052, XKC 053
United Kingdom:	XKC 004, XKC 005, XKC 006, XKC 008, XKC 011, XKC 013, XKC 015, XKC 019, XKC 021, XKC 029, XKC 035, XKC 038, XKC 041, XKC 042, XKC 043, XKC 045, XKC 051
Denmark:	XKC 027
France:	XKC 016
Germany:	XKC 048
Switzerland:	XKC 023
Sweden:	XKC 039
Japan:	XKC 025

C-TYPES TAKING PART IN THE JAGUAR FACTORY CAVALCADE TO LE MANS IN 1991

XKC 008, XKC 015, XKC 021, XKC 025, XKC 027, XKC 028, XKC 029, XKC 035, XKC 036, XKC 038, XKC 039, XKC 042, XKC 043, XKC 051, XKC 052, XKC 053

C-TYPES TAKING PART IN THE JAGUAR FACTORY CAVALCADE TO LE MANS IN 1993

XKC 008, XKC 011, XKC 013, XKC 015, XKC 021, XKC 027, XKC 035, XKC 036, XKC 042, XKC 043, XKC 045, XKC 051, XKC 052, XKC 053

C-TYPES PRESENT AT THE MONTEREY HISTORIC RACE 1992 (FEATURING JAGUAR)

XKC 017, XKC 028, XKC 030, XKC 043, XKC 046, XKC 050

Walker leading a Monopole and an Allard, 1951 Le Mans
Photo ©JDHT

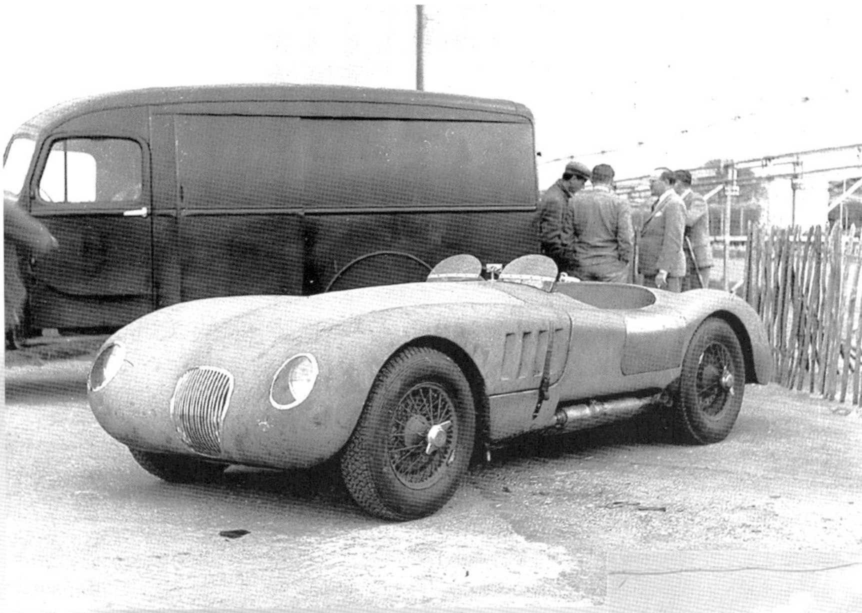

Spring 1951, XKC 001 during tests at Silverstone, still with unlouvred bonnet; 'Lofty' England and Heynes are in the group behind
Photo ©JDHT

The three 1951 Le Mans team cars with Bedford service van, at the old Swallow Road factory before the departure for France
Photo ©JDHT

XKC 001

Chassis number	XKC 001
Distributor	n/a
Current owner	n/a
Engine number	E-1004-8
Registration mark	n/a
Axle ratio	n/a
Body number	n/a
Date of dispatch	n/a
Colour, original	British Racing Green

XKC 001 works car history:

- 1951, Le Mans, driven by Johnson/Biondetti, retired
- 1951, September, Tourist Trophy, Northern Ireland, Johnson/Rolt, fourth, and lap record
- Early 1952, disc brake testing
- *Daily Express* race at Silverstone, driver Rolt, retired
- 1952, August, Goodwood, fitted with new production bonnet, driver Duncan Hamilton, rear hub failed, retired
- 1952, late summer, still with new bonnet, used for *The Motor* magazine road test
- 1953, March, fitted with 1952 long nose bonnet for tests
- 1953, April, taken to Belgium along with production bonnet and used for top speed tests, no significant change in top speeds
- 1953, last known to exist 22 June 1953
- Company paperwork dated 31 August 1953 states: 'dismantled and parts passed to service department'

XKC 002 with the 'long nose' body, before the 1952 Le Mans race
Photo ©JDHT

XKC 002

Chassis number	XKC 002
Distributor	n/a
Current owner	n/a
Engine number	E-1002-8
Registration mark	n/a
Axle ratio	n/a
Body number	n/a
Date of dispatch	n/a
Colour, original	British Racing Green

XKC 002 works car history:

- 1951, Le Mans, Moss/Fairman, retired
- 1951, Tourist Trophy, Moss, first
- 1952, Le Mans, long nose body, Whitehead/Stewart, retired
- 1952, Goodwood 9 Hours, Whitehead/Stewart, crashed
- Last recorded in August 1952; known to have been dismantled at the Jaguar factory

Rear view of XKC 002 with the longer tail, as raced at the 1952 Le Mans
Photo ©JDHT

XKC 003 being prepared for the 1952 Mille Miglia, note the full width windscreen
Photo ©JDHT

Walker going through the Esses, leading an Aston Martin, 1951 Le Mans
Photo Klemantaski/JDHT

XKC 003

Chassis number	XKC 003
Distributor	n/a
Current owner	n/a
Engine number	E-1003
Registration mark	n/a
Axle ratio	n/a
Body number	n/a
Date of dispatch	n/a
Colour, original	British Racing Green

XKC 003 works car history:

- 1951, Le Mans, Walker/Whitehead, first
- 1951, Tourist Trophy, Walker, second
- Early 1952, fitted with disc brakes
- 1952, Easter Goodwood, first race with disc brakes, Moss, fourth and fastest lap
- 1952, Mille Miglia, international disc brake debut, Moss/Dewis, retired
- Monaco GP, Moss, disqualified
- Afterwards, known to have been dismantled at the Jaguar factory

XKC 004

Chassis number	XKC 004
Distributor	Henlys, London, UK
Current owner	Nigel Webb, UK
Engine number	E-1006-8
Registration mark	MDU 214 (original)
Axle ratio	n/a
Body number	K-1006
Date of dispatch	23 May 1952
Colour, original	Pastel Green
Colour, current	British Racing Green

This was the result when Hamilton crashed XKC 004 at Oporto in 1953
Photo ©JDHT

XKC 004 history:

- First privately owned C-type, purchased by Duncan Hamilton
- 1952, Retired in first two races, Isle of Man, 29 May, and Oporto, 22 June
- 1952, August, second to Moss at Boreham and at Turnberry
- IMRC Wakefield, crashed
- 1952, September, Trophy at Carragh
- 1953, June, badly crashed at Oporto
- Car rebuilt and sold to Jack Howey (of Romney, Hythe and Dymchurch Railway) who kept the car for eight years
- Later owners include:
- John Undery, Devon, UK
- Guy Williams, Sussex, UK (late 1960s)
- Stuart Cranfield, Sussex, UK
- C Brierly, Yorkshire, UK
- George Stauffer, Wisconsin, USA
- 1988, sold to Casper McDonald Hall, Hampshire, England
- 2000, sold to Nigel Webb, England

XKC 005

Chassis number	XKC 005
Distributor	Moores, Brighton, UK
Current owner	Humphrey Ernest Avon, UK
Engine number	E-1007-8
Registration mark	MDU 212 (original)
Axle ratio	n/a
Body number	K-1007
Date of dispatch	26 May 1952
Colour, original	Pastel Green
Colour, current	Pastel Green

XKC 005 history:

- First owners Tommy Wisdom and Bill Cannell (of Moores, Jaguar's Brighton distributors)
- Tommy raced it once in the Monaco Grand Prix (race number 82) on 2 June 1952, 94 laps, 183.3 miles. Finishing sixth he became the first private owner to finish a race in a C-type
- It was later fitted with experimental Dunlop disc brakes (with a vacuum servo driven by a Plessey pump off the gearbox) and a compression ratio of 8:1 for Moss, who came in first in a 50 lap race of 224 miles at the Reims Grand Prix meeting on 29 June 1952, averaging 98.18 mph, the first competition success for a disc braked car. He also finished first in the *Daily Mail* International Sports Car Race at Boreham in Essex (88.09 mph), first at Turnberry in Ayrshire (75.36mph), and second (83.02mph) to Tony Rolt in the BARC meeting at Goodwood, setting a new lap record of 85.37mph.
- 1953, loaned to 'works' team, entered in Mille Miglia (25-26 April) driven by Rolt and Len Hayden under race number 638, they retired. Moss finished third in June Goodwood Sports car race, and third in the Goodwood 9 Hour race on 22 August (race number 78)
- September 1953, bought by Brigadier Michael Head. Drum brakes re-fitted, and car painted white. Raced successfully 1954, including a first place at Helsinki Sports car race. First at Lappeenranta, first at Hedemora, a third place in the Johnson Challenge Trophy race at the Goodwood Whitson meeting, and a second place at Snetterton International meeting in August. In March 1955, raced at Goodwood again.
- 1955, sold to Rosemary Vickers (registered FST 777). She won the Ladies' Prize at the Rest-and-Be-Thankful hillclimb. The car was also driven here by John Barber, who won his class. Rosemary Vickers won the Sports Car Handicap at Charterhall on 10 July, but Barber spun and hit the barrier in the Kingsland Trophy Race at Brands Hatch on the Bank Holiday Monday of 1 August
- Later owners include: W Smith, H A Pierpoint, D Head, H M Denton and in 1965 Tony Wood of Northamptonshire, who painted it British Racing Green and had it re-registered under AWW 3; possibly also advertised for sale in *Road and Track* May 1967 by a J C Jamison, La Mesa, California, USA
- 1984, acquired by Humphrey Avon, England. Original experimental Dunlop disc brake refitted, repainted original colour and re-registered as MDU 212. Currently used for historic racing (entry for Le Mans Historic 2001) and shopping!

Starting grid of the sports car race at the 1952 Reims Grand Prix; 'Lofty' England and Stirling Moss (in funny hat) with XKC 005
Photo Talbot Frith/JDHT

XKC 006

Chassis number	XKC 006
Distributor	Rossleigh, Edinburgh, UK
Current owner	David Lake, UK
Engine number	E-1008-8
Registration mark	JWS 353 (original)
Axle ratio	n/a
Body number	K-1008
Date of dispatch	4 July 1952
Colour, original	British Racing Green
Colour, current	Blue

XKC 006 history:

- First Ecurie Ecosse C-type, owned by Ian Stewart
- 1952, very active: Jersey Road Race, first; Charterhall, first (twice); Carragh, first; Castle Coombe, first
- Repainted in the team colour, Metallic Blue
- Goodwood Easter Handicap, Ninian Sanderson sixth
- Ian Stewart then achieved the following: Charterhall and Ibsley, first; Silverstone International, ninth; fourth at Charterhall and first at Snetterton three times
- 1954, sold to Hans David of The Netherlands, raced at Spa and Zandvoort, first; Amiens, second
- 1955, owned by Bryan Corser, used for sprinting. Square bootlid cut in tail
- 1956, Sold to Anthony Barrett-Green of Staffordshire
- 1958, Hammersley of Loughborough, UK
- 1959, Chequered Flag exported the car to David Bevier, New York, USA
- 1961, sold to Robert Allen, New York, USA, used for weekend rides and occasional drives to work
- 1975, returned to the UK and restored by Lynx Engineering for Bill Lake, UK
- Now passed on to David Lake

XKC 006 became the first Ecurie Ecosse car in 1953; here is Ninian Sanderson, in the GoodwoodEaster Handicap race
Photo Guy Griffiths/JDHT

Right: Sir William Lyons with XKC taken at BEN event, 1 July 1978
Photo ©JDHT

WS 353

Phil Hill in XKC 007 at technical inspection, Elkhart Lake, Friday 5 September 1952
Photo courtesy Godfrey Miller

XKC 007

Chassis number	XKC 007
Distributor	Hornburg, Los Angeles, USA
Current owner	Gerald Nell, USA
Engine number	E-1009-8
Registration mark	n/a
Axle ratio	3.54
Body number	K-1009
Date of dispatch	1 August 1952
Colour, original	British Racing Green
Colour, current	British Racing Green

XKC 007 history:

- First C-type to be sent to the USA
- Purchased by Chuck Hornburg who hired Phil Hill to race the car
- With the USA becoming the biggest market for Jaguar, the hope was to promote sales by winning races, which it did
- 1952, September, Elkhart Lake, Hill achieved the first overseas victory for the factory
- 1953, Torrey Pines and Watkins Glenn, Hill, first
- Sold to Carlyle Blackwell, Hollywood, California
- Sold to Robert Lane, California
- Sold to Jack Ratteree, Arizona
- Sold to Walt Osborne
- Sold to Rick Johnson, Arizona, who raced it in several club events and once spun it, going backwards into a cactus
- Bonneville, clocked at 157 mph
- 1986, sold to Terry Larson, Arizona, who restored it
- Sold to Jeffery Pattinson
- Sold to Gerald Nell and used for Concours events in 1993 with several 100 point scores in the Jaguar Club of North America (JCNA) Concours, won national class, and Best Jaguar in JCNA challenge cup winner
- 1996, Meadowbrook, Best Sportscar Award
- 1997, Shown at Pebble Beach, second in class

Phil Hill and Charles Hornburg in XKC 007, Elkhart Lake, 5 September 1952
Photo courtesy Godfrey Miller

XKC 007, by owner Gerald A Nell

I purchased this car in 1993 from Jeffrey Pattinson, who had it stored in Switzerland after purchasing it from Terry Larson. The car was shipped back to Terry, arriving at his business the evening he hosted a cocktail party prior to the Barrett Jackson event in Scottsdale, Arizona. Ironically, all previous owners, as well as myself, were present. Pictures were taken of the group and this significant car. Terry did a complete restoration as it had been raced in Europe while it was there. When it came home to Wisconsin and my garage, it was in concours condition. I chose to show it both in Jaguar Clubs of North America concours d'elegance events where it won many, many first place trophies, and in various prestigious charity concours d'elegance such as Pebble Beach and Meadowbrook. It won trophies at both, including the coveted 'Best Sports Car' award at Meadowbrook.

Although I own a number of significant Jaguars, XKC 007 is one of my favourites. It was never damaged during its racing history in the United States. It will always hold the title of first C-type Jaguar to be shipped to the USA, to win the race (and the last street race) at Elkhart Lake, and to be driven by Phil Hill, who went on to race it in a number of additional races that year. It never lost a race in its racing history. I have retired it from the show circuit, now it will become my 'driver'. Hopefully, I will have as many successful 'touring' miles on it as I do on my 1957 XK-SS which has toured in the USA, England and Europe for more than 15,000 miles – without any serious problems.

I hope to tour some of the highways and byways of the desert and mountains of Southern California and Arizona, before shipping it to England in 2001 where it will take part in the Commemorative Cavalcade from Coventry to Le Mans, celebrating the fiftieth anniversary of the C-type win at Le Mans in 1951. From there it will be shipped to Nashville, Tennessee, to be one of many honoured Jaguars for the Jaguar Clubs of North America 2001 Challenge Championship. During my travels I would very much like to have Phil Hill make a commemorative lap in it, and take his picture some fifty years after its first memorable race with him.

The future world champion Phil Hill changes the plugs on XKC 007 before winning his race at Torrey Pines in 1953. *Photo courtesy Bruce Carnachan.*

XKC 008

Chassis number	XKC 008
Distributor	Direct sale
Current owner	David Wenman, UK
Engine number	E-1011-8
Registration mark	MHP 825 (original)
Axle ratio	4.09
Body number	K-1012
Date of dispatch	26 August 1952
Colour, original	Cream
Colour, current	British Racing Green

XKC 008 works car history:

- Factory prepared for Leslie Johnson, maintained by him, and at Gretton Garage by former Jaguar racing mechanic John Lea, who fitted an overdrive unit for the 1953 Mille Miglia
- Advertised for sale in *Motor Sport* June 1955, September 1958
- Owners include: John Hogg
- John Bekaert, who had several wins and came third in his class in the *Autosport* Championship
- Jackie Epstein did some restoration in the 1960s
- Charles Stoker
- David Merifield
- Patricia Hall
- 1969, Sold to Barclay Wilson
- 1991, Jaguar factory cavalcade to Le Mans
- 1992, Dundrod Classic, second overall
- 1993, Jaguar factory cavalcade to Le Mans
- 1996, Sold to David Wenman, UK
- Special features: Only C-type factory fitted with an overdrive gearbox

XKC 008 with crew, *en route* to the 1953 Mille Miglia *Photo ©JDHT*

George Weaver in XKC 009 (front car) and Phil Hill in XKC 007 (behind) at technical inspection, Elkhart Lake, September 1952
Photo courtesy Godfrey Miller

George Weaver in XKC 009 at Elkhart Lake, September 1952
Photo courtesy Godfrey Miller

XKC 009

Chassis number	XKC 009
Distributor	Hoffman, New York, USA
Current owners	David Darrin Jr., & Drake Darrin, USA
Engine number	E-1010-8
Registration mark	n/a
Axle ratio	3.92
Body number	K-1010
Date of dispatch	1 August 1952
Colour, original	Gunmetal
Colour, current	British Racing Green

XKC 009 history:

- 1952, sent to New York distributor, Max Hoffman
- Prepared by ex-Jaguar mechanic, Jock Reid
- 1952, August, Elkhart Lake, Wisconsin, driver George Weaver
- 1952, Seneca Cup, Watkins Glen, driver John Fitch, first
- 26 October 1952, Turner Air Force Base, Albany, Georgia, driver George Huntoon, first in second race, fourth in main event
- Then sold to first private owner, Dr Wyllie
- 14 March1954, Hunter Air Force Base, Georgia, broke rear axle shaft, did not finish
- Andrews Air Force base, Washington D.C., Dr Wyllie, ninth in third race, fourth in main event
- 16 May 1954, Cumberland, Maryland, fitted latest rear suspension, Margaret 'Peggy' Wyllie, Ladies' race, first; Dr Wyllie, main event, first
- 13 June 1954, Sewickley Hill Climb, Pennsylvania, Dr Wyllie, fastest time of day
- 18 September 1954, Seneca Cup race, Watkins Glen, New York, Dr Wyllie, first
- 31 October 1954, Akron Airport races, Ohio, fifth; Ladies' race, Margaret 'Peggy' Wyllie, first
- 1955, January, car sold to Leech Cracraft, West Virginia, when Dr Wyllie bought XKC 032
- 1955, March, L Cracraft sold XKC 009 to David Darrin, New Jersey
- 7 July 1956, Beverly National Races, Massachusetts, David Darrin, main event, nineteenth
- 19 August 1956, Montgomery Airport races, New York, David Darrin, fourth race, seventh
- These are the only races listed for Darrin in the C- type, most of his races were in a Kaiser-Darrin
- Campaigned extensively at Watkins Glen, Limerock and the Bahamas, including Nassau Speed Week, Tourist Trophy Race, result unknown; loaned to David Albury for Local Residents Race, Heat 1 first, Heat 2 second
- 1983, upon the death of David Darrin, ownership passed to his sons, David Jr. and Drake who campaigned the car at SCCA and USSCA events
- 1992, restored by Bill Bassett, Rhode Island
- 1998, crashed at Watkins Glen, repaired and back in use

Dashboard of XKC 009 taken during technical inspection at Elkhart Lake, September 1952
Photo courtesy Tom Grosteritz

Owner/driver Sherwood Johnston with XKC 010 at Madera, California, 8 November 1952; first race for this car, he finished third. Behind is XKC 007 which Phil Hill drove into second place
Photo courtesy Godfrey Miller

XKC 010

Chassis number	XKC 010
Distributor	Hornburg, Los Angeles, USA
Current owner	Fred Simeone, USA
Engine number	E-1012-8
Registration mark	n/a
Axle ratio	3.54
Body number	K-1013
Date of dispatch	October 2, 1952
Colour, original	Silver
Colour, current	Silver

XKC 010 history:

- Sold (via Hornburg) to Art Feuerbacher of Clayrich Motors, St Louis, the Midwest Jaguar distributor
- 1952, November, Madera, California, Sherwood Johnston drove it to third place
- 1953, best result, March, Sebring 12 Hour race, Johnston and Wilder, third
- Owned for 27 years by Arthur Seyler, Cleveland, Ohio, who raced the C-type in nearly 80 races during his ownership. He removed the original engine for racing, but subsequently replaced it when restoring the car, along with the original shock absorbers and other mechanical parts
- 1991, sold to Fred Simeone, USA

This is believed to be XKC 011 (note louvres in door), driven by Moss at Goodwood in 1953
Photo © JDHT

XKC 011

Chassis number	XKC 011
Distributor	Works car
Current owner	Penny Graham, UK
Engine number	E-1005-8; now E-1066-9
Registration mark	POV 114 (original)
Axle ratio	3.54
Body number	n/a
Date of dispatch	n/a
Colour original	British Racing Green
Colour, current	British Racing Green

Mike Salmon with XKC 011 in 1957
Photo ©JDHT

XKC 011 works car history:

- 1952, May, Silverstone, Peter Walker, retired
- 1952, Le Mans, with long nose body, Moss/Walker, retired
- 1952, Goodwood 9 Hour, Moss/Walker, fifth
- 1952, Shelsley Walsh, Walker, record
- 1952, Prescott, Walker, record
- 1952, Goodwood, Panhard rod fitted, Rolt, first
- 1953, Mille Miglia (with engine number E-1005-8, cylinder head number N.355, 3.31:1 axle, race number 542) Moss/Morris-Goodall, retired
- 1953, Targa Florio, lent to Wisdom, seventeenth
- 1953, Isle of Man British Empire Trophy, Moss (cylinder head number RJ29, S.U. carburettors, 3.54:1 axle, race number 52) second in heat, fourth in final
- Tested with oil cooler
- 1954, January, used for evaluating Avon and Pirelli tyres, Moss favoured Avon
- On loan to Dunlop for testing, repainted Battleship Grey and registered POV 114
- 1957, January, sold by Jaguar to Michael Salmon, a Jaguar employee in the Service Department, repainted Metallic Blue
- 1957 and 1958, extensively campaigned
- 1959, sold to Gordon Lee; for sale in *Motor Sport* April 1963
- Sold to Robin Sturgess, Len Newman and N W Moore
- Repainted British Racing Green
- 1966, sold to Guy Griffiths, Chipping Camden, UK. Later passed on to his daughter Penny Graham, UK, who competed with the car in the late 1960s. The car is still owned by Penny, and used competitively and socially
- 1993, Jaguar factory cavalcade to Le Mans
- 1998, Danish Classic Car Rally and Copenhagen Classic Car Cup street race
- 2000, Copenhagen Classic Car Cup street race

The three 1952 Le Mans cars at the new Browns Lane factory before driving to France. The new admin block is going up in the background
Photo ©JDHT

Moss (driving), and Whitehead (holding the bouquet), with XKC 012, having won the 1953 Reims race *Photo Vachon/JDHT*

XKC 012

Chassis number	XKC 012
Distributor	n/a
Current owner	Tom Groskritz, USA
Engine number	E-1001-8
Registration mark	n/a
Axle ratio	3.54
Body number	n/a
Date of dispatch	n/a
Colour, original	British Racing Green
Colour, current	Not known

XKC 012 works car history:

- 1952, Goodwood 9 Hours, Rolt/Hamilton, crashed after breakage
- 1952, *The Motor* road test car, timed at Jabbeke, 143.75 mph
- 1953, Jabbeke, tested by Norman Dewis, 148.435 mph using Weber carburettors
- 1953, *Daily Express* race at Silverstone, Rolt, (cylinder head number N.352, 4.09:1 axle, Lockheed twin leading-shoe brakes, race number 36), unplaced
- 1953, Le Mans reserve car, driven in practice by Norman Dewis, using team number 18
- 1953, Reims 12 Hours, on loan to Peter Whitehead for himself and Moss (cylinder head number RJ 78, Weber carburettors, 3.31:1 axle, Dunlop disc brakes from XKC 001, new triple plate clutch), race number 4, first
- 1953, Goodwood 9 Hours, Moss/Walker (engine number E-1054, 9:1 compression ratio, 3.92:1 axle), race number 1, retired, number one con. rod broken
- 1953, Tourist Trophy, Whitehead/Stewart, (engine number E-1052, 9:1 compression ratio, 3.54:1 axle), retired, gearbox problems
- 1954, March, engine changed to E1005-8, taken to Le Mans at short notice as substitute for XKC 047 which had crashed en route, rebuilt at Le Mans with parts from XKC 047 and assumed new identity of XKC 047 (see XKC 047)
- Owned by Tom Groskritz, who believes this car is more correctly referred to as XKC 012

The Jaguar pit at Le Mans in 1953, note two cars with race number 18; third from left is XKC 012 which was a practice car.
The Belgian-entered XKC 047 is far right (no. 20)
Photo ©JDHT

XKC 013

Chassis number	XKC 013
Distributor	Hoffman, USA
Current owner	Privately owned, UK
Engine number	E-1013-8
Registration mark	VSU 669
Axle ratio	3.54
Body number	K-1101
Date of dispatch	9 October 1952
Colour, original	Silver with Red interior trim
Colour, current	Metallic Blue

XKC 013 history:

- 25 October 1952, Turner Air Force Base, Georgia, only race by the first owner Robert Blackwood, raced six laps, blew clutch, retired, new clutch installed
- Sold to Frank Miller, New York, who customised the car with a full windscreen, cockpit moulding, and silencer shield
- 1954, March, Sebring, ninth
- 2 May 1954, Andrews Air Force Base, Washington D.C., driver John Gordon Bennett, retired
- Sold to James Lazor of Ohio who kept it for over thirty years before selling it to Anthony Mayman
- Sold to The Hon Alan Clark MP, UK
- Special features: Fog lights fitted in bonnet and D-roll trim on cockpit, louvered panel over exhaust
- 1993, Jaguar factory cavalcade to Le Mans
- 1999, in private ownership following Alan Clark's death

The first owner, John Rutherford, taking XKC 014 to 134mph during NASCAR speed week at Daytona Beach, Florida
Photo ©JDHT

XKC 014

Chassis number	XKC 014
Distributor	Hoffman, New York, USA
Current owner	Skip Barber, USA
Engine number	E-1014-8
Registration mark	XSU 268
Axle ratio	3.92
Body number	K-1014
Date of dispatch	7 October 1952
Colour, original	Cream with Suede Green interior trim
Colour, current	British Racing Green with Green interior trim

XKC 014 history:

- First owner was John Rutherford
- 1953, achieved 134.07 mph at NASCAR Speed Week, Daytona Beach, Florida
- 1960, purchased by David S Burtner who fitted a Valiant slant six, Borg Warner transmission, positraction rear end, and Buick brakes
- Raced extensively in the early 1960s
- Sold to Ralph Steiger for $2,000
- Restored by Peter Jaye and R S Panels for Burkhard von Schenk, Germany
- Sold to Skip Barber, USA

Sherwood Johnston inspects the wreckage as it is unloaded at Hansen McPhee in Boston, after being purchased from Gregory at Floyd Bennett Field
Photo courtesy Godfrey Miller

XKC 015

Chassis number	XKC 015
Distributor	Hornburg, Los Angeles, USA
Current owner	Tom Candlish, UK
Engine number	E-1015-8
Registration mark	TKV 500
Axle ratio	3.92
Body number	K-1015
Date of dispatch	14 October 1952
Colour, original	Cream with Suede Green interior trim
Colour, current	Cream with Suede Green interior trim

XKC 015 history:

- Sold via Hornburg to J Hall who raced it once
- 1953, sold to Masten Gregory who had the following results in 1953:
- 17 May, 100 Mile Guardsman Trophy Race, Golden Gate Nationals, first overall
- 5 July, Offutt Field Nationals, Omaha, Nebraska, first overall
- 12 April, Lone Star 200 mile race, Bergstrum Air Force Base, Austin, Texas, third
- 9 August, Lockbourne Air Force Base, Columbus, Ohio, second
- August, Thompson National, Thompson, Connecticut, first
- August 1953, road tested by *Road and Track*
- Caught fire in an accident, Floyd Bennett Races, New York (Masten Gregory got out OK)
- Sold to Tage Hansen who rebuilt it
- 1954, broke course record, Mount Washington, driven by Sherwood Johnston
- Driven on the road by Hansen for many years
- 1958, sold to Merril Wells of Maine.
- 1961, bought by John Howe of Massachusetts.
- 1964, acquired by Mark Daniels, who carried out an extensive re-build, using bonnet and mid-body sections from 034, which he had bought at about the same time. He used it as a road car and for social rallies until 1979 when he sold it to Godfrey Miller of Vancouver, British Columbia, Canada. Later that year Miller sold it to Campbell McLaren who brought it back to the UK
- 1984 acquired by Tom Candlish, UK. Taken part in all Ecurie Ecosse Scottish rallies since 1989 to date
- 1994, Danish Spring Rally
- 1995, Italia Classica
- 1998, Danish Classic Car Rally and race
- Took part in Jaguar factory cavalcade to Le Mans in 1991 and 1993
- Participant in Le Mans Cavalcade each year from 1994 to present date

Masten Gregory w
John Gordon Ben
on his left see th
proof of the oil le
on XKC 015,
Lockbourne Airfo
base, Columbus,
Ohio, 9 August 1
Photo Godfrey Miller

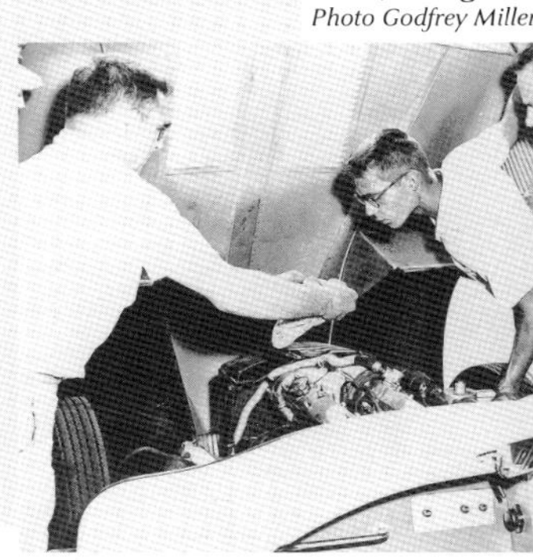

Sherwood Johnston blasts his way up the Mount Washington hill climb in XKC 015 without body for fastest time of day, 15 August 1954
Photo Godfrey Miller

Masten Gregory in XKC 015 takes the checkered flag from starter Terry Field, at Offut Field, Omaha, Nevada 5 July 1953; 200 miles at 76.6 mph
Photo Godfrey Miller

XKC 016

Chassis number	XKC 016
Distributor	Delecroix, Paris, France
Current owner	Philippe Renault, France
Engine number	E-1016-8
Registration mark	n/a
Axle ratio	3.54
Body number	K1016
Date of dispatch	16 October 1952
Colour, original	Special Blue with Red interior trim
Colour, current	Special Blue

XKC 016 history:

- Sold via Delecroix, Paris, to Lyon Dealer, Henri Peignaux
- 1953, March, fastest Montlhéry, Soleil-Cannes Rally test but crashed when trailing arm broke
- 1953, crashed by Descollanges in Mille Miglia, co-driver Ugnon killed
- History afterwards unknown, until re-discovered many years later by Philippe Renault, France

Sterling Edwards in XKC 017 at Torrey Pines, 1952
Photo courtesy Bruce Carnachan

XKC 017

Chassis number	XKC 017
Distributor	Hornburg, Los Angeles, USA
Current owner	Terry Larson, USA
Engine number	E-1017
Registration mark	857 L
Axle ratio	3.54
Gearbox number	JH11669
Chassis complete	25 August 1952
Archives card no.	32406
Body number	K-1017
Date of dispatch	7 October 1952
Colour, original	Birch Grey with Red interior trim
Colour, current	Black with Red interior trim

XKC 017 history:

- Supplied to Hornburg, Los Angeles, USA
- Sold first to Sterling Edwards, San Francisco, California
- XKC 017 had considerable racing success in the 1950s, including:
- 1952, third at Torrey Pines, California
- While the car was still owned by Sterling Edwards, it was also driven by Irv Robbins in races including Palm Springs
- Crashed by mechanic at Pebble Beach (hit a hay bale)
- 1953, sold to Lou Brero
- 1953, air scoops fitted for better brake cooling
- 1954, fifth at March Field, Riverside, California
- First in the first Torrey Pines 6 Hour Endurance Race
- Lou Brero also did very well in other races as well as hill climbs in California
- 1955, sold to Ray Seher, Nevada
- Ray raced it over the next two years, including:
- 1955, third at Santa Rosa, California
- 1955, Sacramento, California. Four trophies in one day with five victories including:
- First in class, second overall; first overall; first in class, second overall
- 1955, Stockton, California, first
- 1955, Kotati Air Field, California, first
- 1956, Salinas, California, first in class, and first overall
- Santa Rosa, California, first
- Kotati Air Field, California, second
- Raced at Walnut Grove and Stockton California
- Laguna Seca, California, third
- Sold to Leon Mandel, the publisher of *Autoweek magazine*
- Mandel raced in Northern California about six times

Lou Brero after winning the first Torrey Pines 6 hour endurance race in 1954. He held off the second placed car for the last 2 hours with a broken right axle upper link!
Photo courtesy Terry Larson

y Seher in XKC 017 at ckton, California, 18 March 55; first in class and first erall
oto Terry Larson

XKC 017 cont...

- Also raced by Bob Bryan
- 1961, Golden Gate Park Race, driver Bob Potter, second
- Sold to Chuck Davies during the above race
- Davies then restored the car for Concours and daily use. He did very well in several Concours including:
- 1962, Hillsboro, California, second
- 1963, Santa Rosa, California, first
- 1963, Palo Alto, California, first
- 1964, Pebble Beach, California, first
- 1967, featured in January issue of *Road and Track* magazine
- 1969, sold to Orin Palmer, San Jose, California
- 1970, raced at Laguna Seca, California
- Then sat in storage until 1987, when it was sold to Terry Larson
- Raced extensively since, including:
- 1987, ASRA, FIR, Phoenix, Arizona, first in class; JCNA Slalom, Laguna Seca, California, first overall
- 1988, 1989 and 1990: ASRA, Phoenix
- 1991: 18 February, ASRA, Phoenix, first in class; 10 August, Monterey Pre-Historics, California; 19 August, Monterey Historics, eleventh overall; 19 September, VARA, Willow Springs, California, first in class
- 1992: 19 August, Monterey Historics, second overall, and Monterey Historic Award; 10 October, VARA, PIR, Phoenix, first in class; 4 December, VARA, Willow Springs, first in class, and VARA Class Champion
- 1993: 13 February, ASRA, Phoenix; 20 February, VARA, Phoenix, second in class; 20 August, Monterey Historics, second overall; 5 November, VARA, Las Vegas, Nevada, third in class; 5 December, VARA, Willow Springs, second in class
- 1994: 20 August, Monterey Pre-Historics, second overall
- 1995: 25 February, VARA, Phoenix, third overall; 18 August, Monterey Historics, third overall
- 1996: 15 August, Monterey Historics, fifth overall; November, VARA, Las Vegas, first in class
- 1997: 18 April, VARA, Buttonwillow, California, first in class; 14 August, Monterey Historics, second overall (to Phil Hill)
- 1998: 28 March, HMSA, Monterey; 29 November, VARA, Phoenix, first place
- 1999: 19 February, VARA, Phoenix, third in class; 21 May, Wine Country Classic, Sears Point, California, DNF (leading race when axle snapped); 20 August, Monterey Pre-Historics, second overall; 27 August, Monterey Historics, fourth overall; 22 October Coronado Speed Festival, California, third overall
- 2000: 1 April, HMSA, Monterey, second overall; 11 August, Monterey Pre-Historics, second overall; 18 August, Monterey Historics, eight overall; 10 October, Coronado Speed Festival, first overall in both races ('crew chief' Norman Dewis)
- Special features: air scoops fitted in 1953 by Lou Brero for brake cooling

XKC 017, by owner Terry Larson

I found and purchased XKC 017 in 1987 after it had been sitting in storage for seventeen years. When I first saw the car, I had no way of knowing how attached I would become. C-types do seem to have that effect on people.

XKC 017 was raced very hard early in its life, with much success. One of the things that I enjoy about my car is that when I go to race meetings, I always hear stories from people who have worked on it, taken period photos, or just know of its history. The brake scoops, which were neatly fitted by Lou Brero on the tail section in 1953, make it easy to identify.

While racing at Buttonwillow, California, someone walked up to me and said 'That's the old Sterling Edwards car, isn't it?' He remembered the car from when he was ten years old in its first race. His father was in the same group, and he sent me a photo with the race programme.

That same year at the Monterey Historics, I qualified on the first row with Phil Hill in another Lou Brero car (375MM Ferrari) and was wished good luck by Lou Brero's daughter and Ray Seher's daughter (who was a flag person on the circuit). Ray and Lou both did well with XKC 017. When Lou won the first Torrey Pines 6 Hour Endurance Race he held off the second place car for two hours having a broken rear axle upper link. Since this is what keeps the rear axle from moving from side to side, he went through three sets of rear tyres from rubbing on the chassis. It is hard to imagine what an adventure that must have been!

In 1988 Dutch Mandel (editor of Autoweek Magazine*) spoke at a Jaguar Club banquet telling the story of how when he was a baby, his mother would take him for a ride in the mountains in XKC 017 to help put him to sleep. Years later, I arranged for Dutch and his father Leon to be re-united with this car for the Copperstate 1000. As Dutch slipped into the seat, I commented 'It is probably a bit more tight that the last time you were in there.' Past owners are, after all, part of the history and 'heart and soul' of these cars. We do not really own our cars, we are the caretakers while we are here. There have been many fond memories with this car – these are only a few of them.*

XKC 018

Chassis number	XKC 018
Distributor	Bourgeois, Belgian Motor Company, Belgium
Current owner	Bruce Lustman, USA
Engine number	E-1018-8
Registration mark	n/a
Axle ratio	3.54
Body number	K-1018
Date of dispatch	27 October 1952
Colour, original	Bronze with Silver interior trim
Colour, current	Bronze

XKC 018 history:

- Sold to Juan Manuel Fangio who immediately re-sold it to Jose Millet (the local Jaguar Distributor) of Buenos Aires, Argentina
- 1953, first raced at Mendoza in June, finishing third
- Sold to Mr Magnasco
- 1958, sold to Jose Millet who kept the car for several years
- 1979, sold to Ernesto Tornquist
- 1983, sold to Bill Tracy
- 1997, sold to Georgio Acutis, West Indies, and kept by Veniero Molari, Italy
- 2001, car sold through R M Auctions, Arizona, to Bruce Lustman

Opposite page
Top:
XKC 017 with bonnet up at Salinas, California, 1956; driven by Ray Seher to first in class and first overall *Photo courtesy Terry Larson*
Bottom:
The dashboard of XKC 017 *Photo courtesy Terry Larson*
Above:
Although it is Paul Frere behind the wheel of XKC 018, this was the car sold to Fangio - one of three world champions who chose Jaguar *Photo ©JDHT*

XKC 019

This picture was probably taken in the 1960's when XKC 019 was owned DeGroo in Holland *Photo ©JDHT*

Chassis number	XKC 019
Distributor	Bourgeois, Belgium Motor Company, Belgium
Current owner	Clinton Bourke, UK
Engine number	E-1019-8
Registration mark	UFF 376
Axle ratio	3.54
Body number	K-1019
Date of dispatch	24 October 1952
Colour, original	Silver
Colour, current	British Racing Green

XKC 019 history:

- The first owner was Herman Roosdorp of Antwerp, Belgium
- 1953, Spa 24 Hour race, driven by Roosdorp/Ulmen, third overall, best result for Roosdorp
- 1953, Nürburgring 1000km Race, Roosdorp/Ulmen, retired, Ulmen crashed
- 1953, September, Roosdorp recorded 234 kph (145.4 mph) at Jabbeke but did not break record
- Sold to J L van Dieten, The Hague
- 1954, Zandvoort, van Dieten placed fifth
- 1959, Hans Maasland, Netherlands
- 1962, Jan Bos-Eyssen, Netherlands, painted Old English White
- 1965, Piet de Groot, Amsterdam, Maserati dealer
- December 1967, advertised for sale in *Road and Track* by Herb Watson (dealer), New York, as 'just imported from Europe', for $6000.
- 1968, sold to Preston Smith, Pennsylvania
- Returned to Europe in 1984 by Gerhard Hage
- Subsequent owners included:
- 1990, Eckart Berg
- 1991, Peter Groh
- 1991, Hans Schede, of British Motors (dealers), Germany
- 1993, sold to Hugh Taylor, UK
- 1995, sold to Hugh Palmer, UK
- 1997, sold to Clinton Bourke, UK
- 1999, Mille Miglia Storica (and three previous entries in this event)

XKC 019, by owner Clinton Bourke

One of the many great advantages of owning an XK Jaguar is the opportunity to enter what is arguably the world's greatest classic event, the Italian Mille Miglia Storica. Each year more than 800 applicants are reduced to an entry list of around 370 vehicles, all produced between 1927 and 1957, the years between which the famous road race was held twenty-three times.

The year 1999 saw twenty-three British entries, with eleven from Jaguar. All the Coventry cars finished although one was unclassified, and two Jaguar-engined 'specials' also made it back to Brescia. My own car, XKC 019, had previously completed the gruelling course of around 1000 miles in the hand of three previous owners, and I am pleased to report that she maintained her reliability record. Throughout, the C-type behaved impeccably, checking of fluid levels required no action, and at the end, just half a litre of oil was all that was needed.

Allocated number 306, my Italian navigator Gabrielle Fabbri and I left Brescia at just before 10.00pm on Thursday 6 May and arrived at Ferrara around 2.00am on Friday morning. After three hours' sleep, we were on the road again at 8.41am with just thirteen hours motoring to Rome. Saturday, the final and most demanding day, saw us depart from Rome at 8.11am and arrive, 400 miles later, in Brescia at just after 11.00pm. As seems to be the modern norm at some stage of the event, heavy rain set in from Bologna, through Modena and on to the finish, and these miles in the dark in the heavy rush hour traffic, were the least pleasurable.

In the end we were rewarded with 191st position which compared with Moss in 104th, Sandro Munari (twelve times World Rally Champion) in 148th, Roger Penske in 226th, Jochen Mass in 232nd and Jose Carreras in 237th position, all in works supported Mercedes-Benz models.

En route, the round trip had provided memorable scenery via roads not normally open to public traffic, through the historic locations of Ferrara, San Marino, Assisi, Radicofani and Florence. In the mountains, the Ferraris, Maseratis and Stirling Moss in the Mercedes-Benz 300 SLR (number 300) had to use their gearboxes to maintain speed, whist in the C-type we held second or third as appropriate, and used the tremendous torque to maintain a respectable position.

Equally unforgettable as the vistas that opened around each corner, was the reaction from the enthusiastic Italian crowds. They were unbelievable with their support, cheering not just the patriotic red entrants – our own Jaguar was well received everywhere we went. I have never experienced anything like the Mille Miglia. It is memorable for a multitude of reasons, including the (at times) chaotic and frustrating organisation, or rather the lack of it.

Now that the fatigue of competing has passed, I am better able to appreciate and savour the special moments from an historic journey, marvel at the exploits of Nuvolari who won in 1930 and 1933, and Stirling Moss who set the highest ever average speed of 156 km per hour and won in 1955 – all this achieved on mostly unsurfaced roads, open to the public.

The start at Zandvoort in 1954, with five C-types in the line up *Photo courtesy Clinton Bourke*

XKC 020

Chassis number	XKC 020
Distributor	Hoffman, New York, USA
Current owner	n/a, car stolen in the 1970s
Engine number	E-1020-8
Registration mark	n/a
Axle ratio	3.54
Body number	K-1020
Date of dispatch	9 October 1952
Colour, original	Silver
Colour, current	British Racing Green

XKC 020 history:

- Sold via the Imported Car Company of Hoopeston, Illinois, to Frank Larson
- 1953, Bergstrom Air Force Base, Texas, first listed race, Frank Larson, first race eighth, fourth race fifth
- 14 June1953, Chanute Air Force Base, Illinois, Dr John Urbas, second
- 4 July 1953, Offutt Air Force Base, Nebraska, Frank Larson, second race, third, Dr. John Urbas, fourth race, third
- 1953 July 26, Wilmot Hills race, Wisconsin, Fred Wacker, first
- Sold to Guy Mabee, Texas
- 1954, Carroll Shelby raced it upon return from Europe, including two wins in Texas
- 28 March 1954, Bergstrom Air Force Base, fourth race, third
- 1954, late summer, Fort Worth Air Force Base, SCCA regional race, first
- 1955, W L Petrie, Houston, Texas, bought the car and fitted a Chevrolet V8 engine, Dunlop disc brakes and Halibrand disc knock off wheels
- 1956, sold to Carroll Shelby Sports Cars, Texas
- 1957, July, Galveston, Texas, driver Mason O'Kieff, fifth
- 1958, November, Hammond Harvest races, Louisiana, O'Kieff, third
- Sold to Herb Stetler, Louisiana
- 1960, April, driven by A J Foyt at Riverside in practice, did not race
- Sold to Tom Dreyfus, New Orleans, Louisiana
- Car stolen in the 1970's and has not been seen since. However, the engine has since turned up in Texas; the original engine was not in the car at the time the car was stolen

XKC 021

Chassis number	XKC 021
Distributor	Appleyards, Leeds, UK
Current owner/keeper	Ben Cussons, UK
Engine number	E-1021-8
Registration mark	PUG 676
Axle ratio	3.92
Body number	K-1021
Date of dispatch	23 September 1952
Colour, original	Suede Green
Colour, current	Not known

XKC 021 history:

- May have been used by Ian Appleyard
- Sold via Leeds distributor to Bill Holt in time for September Goodwood Meeting
- 1953 and 1954, Raced by Bill Holt and Mike Connell but without any great success
- 1954, February, work done by factory when mileage was 4,624. Fitted with ex-HWM engine
- 1954, May, sold to Mike Connell, Norfolk
- Returned to factory when mileage was 8,164
- Sold to David Boston, Liverpool
- 1955, March, Goodwood, third, shared by Dick Protheroe and David Boston
- 1956, April, sold to Maberyl Parker, Wales
- 1960, sold to Mike Richardson
- 1960, Bill MacKay raced it in the Scottish Speed Championship
- Sold to Hillhead Auto Company, Glasgow
- 1961, January, sold to Kenneth Moore, Middlesex
- 1961, August, advertised in *Motor Sport* and sold to John Buncombe, Burnham-on-Sea
- 1962, September, owned by Ronald Bateman, Inverness, registered ARB 3
- 1965, April, purchased by John Hallihan
- 1966, sent to Australia for restoration, re registered TST 225
- Sold to Bill Marshall
- Purchased by David Lomas, UK, and re registered YSV 242, later reverted to PUG 676
- 1991,1993 Jaguar factory cavalcade to Le Mans
- Bad crash in 1999 Tour de France with Ben Cussons who is the current keeper

XKC 022

Chassis number	XKC 022
Distributor	Hoffman, New York, USA
Current owner	David Rubin, USA
Engine number	E-1022-8
Registration mark	n/a
Axle ratio	3.54
Body number	K1022
Date of dispatch	28 October 1952
Colour, original	Red with Silver interior trim
Colour, current	Not known

XKC 022 history:

- Originally sold to Henry W Wessels who raced it on a number of occasions:
- 22 February 1953, MacDill Air Force Base, Tampa, Florida, ninth place in Formula race
- 30 May 1953, Thompson Raceway, Connecticut, third
- 9 August 1953, Lackbourne Air Force Base, Ohio, fourth race, retired last lap; fifth race, twelfth on handicap
- 29 August 1953, Floyd Bennett Field races, New York, practised Saturday only. Wessells then sold the car to Masten Gregory who raced it on Sunday but retired
- 6 September 1953, Thompson Raceway, Connecticut, sixth race, Masten Gregory, first
- 8 November 1953, March Air Force Base, Riverside, California, novice race, Ridelle Gregory first, main event Masten Gregory, fourth
- 24 January 1954, Buenos Aires, Argentina, 1000km race, race number18, Masten Gregory with co-driver Dale Duncan, car fitted with 40mm Weber carburettors, water pump belt broke, did not finish
- 1954, September, Kansas City, Missouri, car repainted red, seats reupholstered
- Advertised for sale for $6,000 with trailer of spare parts, sold to James Hall, Texas
- 1955, July, advertised for sale for $4,250
- 1956, sold to William Wilson, New Orleans, four races, two wins and class win
- 1963, sold to David Rubin, USA, for $750.00. Still owned by him, and is still in good restorable condition

Top:
XKC 022 in the pit at McDill Air Force Base, Tampa, Florida, 19 February 1953 *Photo courtesy Godfrey Miller*
Middle:
Interior and dashboard of XKC 022 *Photo courtesy Tom Groskritz*
Bottom:
XKC 022 at speed at McDill Air Force Base, Tampa, Florida, 19 February 1953 *Photo courtesy Terry Larson*

XKC 023

Chassis number	XKC 023
Distributor	Hornburg, Los Angeles USA
Current owner	Christian Jenny, Switzerland
Engine number	E-1023-8
Registration mark	n/a
Axle ratio	3.54
Body number	K-1023
Date of dispatch	28 November 1952
Colour, original	Red
Colour, current	Red

XKC 023 history:

- Charles Hornburg sold XKC 023 to Seattle Jaguar dealer Joe Henderson
- 1953, August, Seattle Seafair 100 Mile race, driven by Jack Douglas and Bill Pollack, second
- 10 July 1955, Torrey Pines, California, Jack Douglas rolled the car. XKC 033 (Tom Groskritz) and XKC 024 (Pearce Woods) were also in this race
- Engine fitted with a new C-type cylinder head
- Sold to Ces Critchlow, Huntington Beach, California, who owned an auto repair shop
- 18 November 1956, Paramount Ranch race, Ces rolled XKC 023
- Sold to Horvath Motors, Costa Mesa, California. The body was considered too badly damaged for repair, it was decided to fit a Devin fibreglass body which was inexpensive and made in California
- 1961, Horvath Motors traded XKC 023 in exchange for painting their building
- 1962, Frank Schierenbeck, who owned Car Service Imported, on Harbor Boulevard, Costa Mesa, California, took the car in trade for an engine rebuild. When Frank got the car it was together and complete, needing a bit of electrical and mechanical work, which he did
- 1962, Frank had the car inspected by the Motor Vehicle Department, and registered for road use
- 1963, Frank was clocked at 165 mph at Orange County Airport
- XKC 023 sat in storage at Frank's home until 1997
- 1997, sold to Terry Larson, then to Christian Jenny, Switzerland
- Restored for Christian Jenny by Terry Larson

XKC 023 drive by Jack Douglas at Bakersfield, California,1 May 1955
Photo courtesy Terry Larson

XKC 023, by owner Christian J Jenny

My car, XKC 023, has had a most important and varied life and even more, is known to be the last re-discovered C-type. A 'barn find' by Arizona-based C- and D-type expert and Jaguar restoration professional Terry Larson, this C-type had been owned for 35 years by one single owner, longer than most other C-types.

From the late sixties until 1997, the whereabouts of XKC 023 had vanished into obscurity. At last, it stood out as the only one of the 53 C-types produced that remained unaccounted for. In the mid-1980s, Terry first became aware of Frank Schierenbeck and his collection of XKs, remaining in various stages of disassembly, stacked away in a number of sheds in Northern California. For more than ten years they would talk on the 'phone until in late 1997, Terry went to his place and first sighted the scattered pieces belonging to XKC 023. Recounting the discovery, he says 'We're not talking about a few little bits, we're talking about everything you need to drive down the road.' Moreover, he found the original stamped identification number XKC 023 on the front cross member, one of two places where the chassis numbers had originally been located.

Clearly, there were the parts of a complete car, the original chassis, original engine block with matching number, original gearbox, all other important parts, even the original footwells – of course with the exception of the body, missing and replaced by a Devin body. Larson purchased it all for his client, Christian Jenny. When starting the re-assembly, he became aware that one of the body mounts to fit the Devin body was welded over the spot on the shock tower where the original chassis number was supposed to be. It had remained untouched for the past 40 years. The process of cutting the weld and folding back the body mount was meticulously recorded on film. Without any doubt, what appeared was the original number XKC 023: Final proof that he had indeed obtained the original chassis.

Those parts of the original body, wrecked in 1957, which had remained unbent, eventually found their way into a complete car, built on an original factory C-type replacement chassis. This replica 'of higher order' (or 'spares car') was purchased by Jenny and Larson in order to remove the original body parts and have them reunited with XKC 023. Subsequently the 'spares car' was sold as a replica, with the original factory un-numbered chassis.

An original C-type bonnet and tail section already owned by Terry Larson, together with the parts taken from the 'spares car', were sent to RS Panels in Coventry, England, to rebuild the complete C-type body. After returning, restoration continued at Terry's shop in Mesa, Arizona. All parts were thoroughly cleaned and tested, block, head, carburettors, gearbox, and a great many other parts underwent a complete rebuild. C-type disc brakes were installed in place of the less reliable drum brakes, although not the disc brakes of a lightweight C-type. A new radiator, electrical wiring and components were installed, and eventually it was all re-assembled into the original C-type that it is today. It was painted again in the original red that it was in 1952.

In late October 2000, XKC 023 underwent a thorough 800 mile test on the C- and D-type tour to Northern Arizona organised by the Larsons. On that occasion, it ran without any problems and was pronounced fit, 'checked and passed', by former Chief Test Engineer of Jaguar Cars, Norman Dewis.

XKC 023 with rear end damage at Paramount Raceway, California, 18 November 1956, owner Ces Critchlow (wearing glasses) behind car *Photo courtesy Terry Larson*

XKC 024

Chassis number	XKC 024
Distributor	Hornburg, Los Angeles, USA
Current owner	Fred Bohlander, USA
Engine number	E-1024-8
Registration mark	878 FUF
Axle ratio	3.54
Body number	K-1024
Date of dispatch	24 November 1952
Colour, original	British Racing Green
Colour, current	British Racing Green with Green interior trim

XKC 024 history:

- 1953, April; the first owner, Alex Thompson of Colorado had Phil Hill drive the car to an excellent second place behind Jim Kimberly, Ferrari, and in front of Masten Gregory, XKC 015, at the Lone Star 200 mile race at Bergstrom Air Force Base, Austin, Texas
- Purchased by James Harrison, Colorado Springs, Nevada, a Jaguar dealer
- 8 November 1953, Harrison crashed at the East vs. West meeting, March Field, Riverside, California. New chassis, centre body section and bonnet. Damaged bonnet used on XKC 031
- 10 July 1955, Torrey Pines, Pearce Woods, did not finish
- Also raced by Harold Erb
- Sold to dealers in San Diego
- Sold to Jim Kirk, Palasades, California
- 1980, sold to Peter Agg, Surrey, UK who kept it until 1982
- Sold to Bob Reid, Geneva
- 1988 and 1989, Restored by John Pearson and R S Panels UK
- Sold to Jim Wallis, UK
- 1994 sold to Dalle Carbonare, Italy
- 1997 sold to Fred Bohlander, USA

XKC 025

Chassis number	XKC 025
Distributor	Moto Maroc, Casablanca, Morocco
Current owner	Mr Naito, Japan
Engine number	E-1025-8
Registration mark	XSV 894
Axle ratio	3.54
Body number	K-1025
Date of dispatch	19 January 1953
Colour, original	British Racing Green
Colour, current	Blue

XKC 025 history:

- Supplied to Moto Maroc, Casablanca, Morocco
- Sold to Armand Roboly
- 1953, Hyeres 12 Hour race in France with John Simone driving, second
- Tour de France, retired
- Later in USA
- 1962, reported to have been seen at Stuckers Auto Parts, Staten Island, New York, for sale for $300.00
- 1962, purchased from Stuckers Auto Parts, Staten Island, New York, by Al Lendzion, New Jersey (later Florida)
- 1976, advertised in *Hemmings Motor News* by Al Lendzion for $800.00 or swap for 1949 Buick Coupe, picture shows full rolling chassis but no body, engine or gearbox
- Sold to Ali Lugo, then John Handshy, Connecticut
- Sold overseas and restored by Hall and Fowler, UK, in 1990 and 1991. Registered XSV 894
- Owned by Hubertus Graf von Donhoff, Germany
- 1991, Jaguar factory cavalcade to Le Mans
- 1992, sold to Paul Burdell, UK
- 1994, sold to David Cohen, Canada
- 1997, sold to Japanese collector, Mr Naito

Opposite page left:
XKC 024 as wrecked by James Harrison of Colorado Springs, on March Field, California, 1953
Photo courtesy Terry Larson
Middle and top:
XKC 024 at Santa Barbara Airport races, California, September 1955, in two-tone colour scheme
Photo courtesy Fred Bohlander
Right:
XKC 025 with owner Armand Roboly (at the wheel) and his co-driver John Simone for the start of the 1953 Tour de France
Photo courtesy Terry Larson

XKC 026

Chassis number	XKC 026
Distributor	Hornburg, Los Angeles, USA
Current owner	Jack Croul, USA
Engine number	E-1026-8
Registration mark	n/a
Axle ratio	3.54
Body number	K-1026
Date of dispatch	24 November 1952
Colour, original	Cream
Colour, current	Cream

XKC 026 history:

- Kjell Qvale at British Motor Car Distributors, San Francisco sold the car to fiction writer Al Coppel
- 1953, picture of car with Al Coppel on cover of *Road and Track*
- 1953, sold to Sterling Edwards
- Madera, California, was second behind Phil Hill in 2.9 Ferrari and ahead of Masten Gregory in a 4.1 Ferrari
- Edwards started driving for Ferrari and sold the car to Julio Mariscal, Mexico City who replaced the S.U. carburettors with Webers
- Imported from Mexico by Jon Ward, California, minus interior but otherwise complete with a repaired body
- Sold to James Rodgers, Tennessee, who had some work done in Chicago
- Sold to George Gillette, Denver, USA, who had Hill and Vaughan restore the car in 1990
- 1991, car did not sell at Pebble Beach, California
- 1992, sold to John Coombs, Monaco. Now with correct S.U. carburettors.
- 1996, sold to Jack Croul, USA

Sterling Edwards in XKC 026, Golden Gate Park 1953. *Photo courtesy Webb Canepa.*

No less than William Lyons and 'Lofty' England, in a rare colour photo taken at the 1952 Elkhart Lake race
Photo ©JDHT

Tom Candlish enjoying XKC 015, now registered TKV 500
Photo courtesy Tom Candlish

Present owner Tom Candlish in XKC 015, followed by a D-type (owned by Ole Sommer)
Photo courtesy Tom Candlish

The interior and dashboard of XKC 032 to-day
Photo courtesy Julio Palmaz

Ray Seher in XKC 017 at Sacramento co
fairgrounds, October 1955. The car clipp
strawbales but righted itself, and Ray fir
third
Photo courtesy Terry Larson

XKC 042 restored in the Ecurie Ecosse colours, driven by present owner Dick Skipworth
Photo courtesy Dick Skipworth

Stirling Moss at Le Mans in 1953, driving XKC 053 which finished second
Photo ©JDHT

The engine of XKC 032 to-day
Photo courtesy Julio Palmaz

The freshly-restored XKC 023 in Arizona
Photo courtesy Christian Jenny

The restored XKC 023 in a wintry setting
Photo courtesy Christian Jenny

XKC 001 in the factory yard before the 1951 T.T. at Dundrod where it was driven by Johnson and Rolt into fourth place
Photo ©JDHT

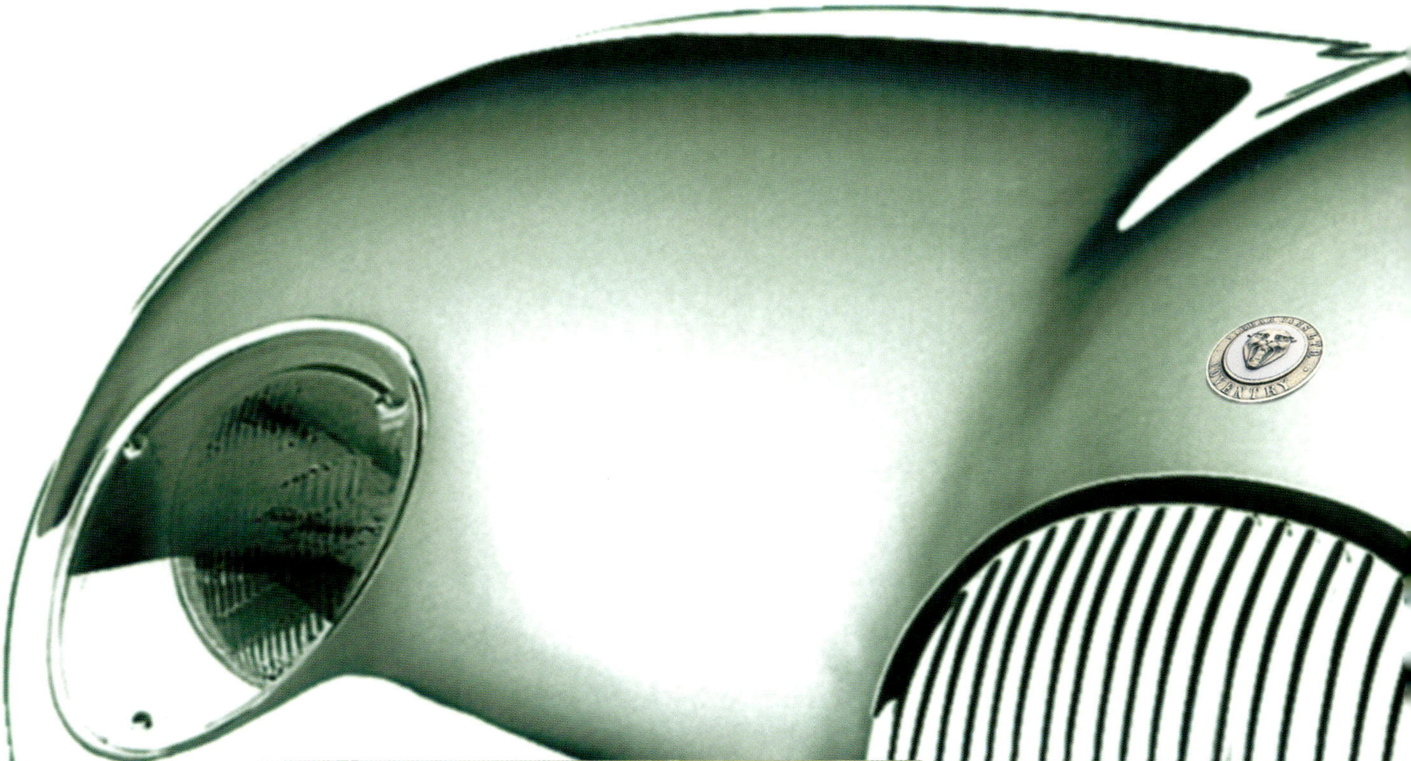

The 1953 Le Mans winner, XKC 051, as owned by Adrian Hamilton to-day, here at a Louis Vuitton ***concours d'elegance***
Photo courtesy Christian Jenny

XKC 032 to-day in the ownership of the Palmaz family
Photo courtesy Julio Palmaz

XKC 048 in action at a recent German event
Photo courtesy Stanislaus Donhoff

XKC 023 at Santa Barbara before it was rebodied in1956; the driver is unknown.
Photo courtesy CorsaResearch.

This picture is believed to be John Simone, driving at Montlhery on 12 April 1953
Photo ©JDHT

XKC 027

Chassis number	XKC 027
Distributor	Marcel Fleury, Geneva, Switzerland
Current owner	Ole Sommer, Denmark
Engine number	E-1027-8
Registration mark	E 11413, now OS
Axle ratio	3.54
Body number	K-1027
Date of dispatch	15 January 1953
Colour, original	Cream
Colour, current	Green

XKC 027 history:

- 1953, February, sold to John Simone, a former USAF Colonel who received the Legion d'Honneur for his French Resistance efforts
- Agadir Grand Prix, third; Marrakesh Grand Prix, second
- 1953, October, sold to Jacques Jonneret, Geneva
- 1954, Nimes Grand Prix, France, first; Bern Grand Prix, Switzerland, fourth; Barcelona Grand Prix, Spain, fourth; Montlhéry Grand Prix, France, second; also first place four times, second place twice, and one third place in hill climbs in France, Italy, and Switzerland; Geneva Rally, crashed
- 1954, December, sold to Paul R Vogel, Geneva
- 1955, various hill climbs in Switzerland, second place three times, and two third places; Grand Prix des Frontieres, Chimay, Belgium, retired while lying third
- 1962, sold back to Marcel Fleury, Switzerland
- 1975, sold to Ole Sommer, Denmark; registered in Denmark under the personal registration mark OS
- 1991 and 1993, Jaguar factory cavalcades to Le Mans
- 2000, Copenhagen Classic Car Cup street race

XKC 028

Chassis number	XKC 028
Distributor	Hornburg, Los Angeles, USA
Current owner	Philippe Reyns, USA
Engine number	E-1028-8
Registration mark	n/a
Axle ratio	O3.54
Body number	K-1028
Date of dispatch	24 November 1952
Colour, original	Silver
Colour, current	Silver with Blue interior trim

XKC 028 history:

- Sold by Hornburg to Jaguar dealer in Denver, Colorado, Kurt Kirchner
- Sold to Doug Maier, Cleveland, Ohio who drove it 23,000 miles
- 1968, sold to William Franz, Ohio
- 1974, sold to Pat Black who started restoration
- 1981, sold to Joe Egle
- 1981, Atlanta Vintage Grand Prix, raced for the first time, came in first overall
- Joe Egle raced the car extensively including Road America and Monterey, until 1988
- 1985, driven on the parade lap of Kansas City Follies Grand Prix by Phil Hill and Masten Gregory
- 1988, Sold to Bob Baker, Nebraska who used the car in many events including the Colorado Grand, Laguna Seca and Sears Point
- 1991, Jaguar factory cavalcade to Le Mans
- 1992, Monterey historic C-type race
- 1995, sold to Philippe Reyns, USA, and used in vintage events on a regular basis
- 1996, Monterey Historics, fourteenth overall
- 2000, Wine Country Classic, first overall

XKC 028 being delivered by United Airlines at Cleveland Airport
Photo courtesy Terry Larson

XKC 029

Chassis number	XKC 029
Distributor	Hornburg, Los Angeles, USA
Current owner	Alan Dunkerley, UK
Engine number	E-1029-8
Registration mark	JSV 258
Axle ratio	3.54
Body number	K-1029
Date of dispatch	24 November 1952
Colour, original	Pastel Green
Colour, current	British Racing Green with Green interior trim

XKC 029 history:

- Re-exported from California to Mexico
- 1953, Carrera Pan Americana, driven by Paco Ibarra, entry sponsored by the 'Estado de Mexico', retired early with engine trouble
- 1954, sold to Javier Velazques, production manager of Automoviles Ingleses, SA, Mexico City (not Jaguar agents)
- 1954, Carrera Pan Americana, sponsored by 'Veracruz'. Believed to be the only C-type to have competed in the original Carrera series
- Reappeared many years later in Massachusetts, USA, owned by William Frey
- Sold to Brian Classic, UK
- Sold to C Brierley
- 1981, purchased by Alan Dunkerley, UK. Rebuilt and registered JSV 258
- 1989, took part in Manx Classic, but mainly used non-competitively
- 1991, Jaguar factory cavalcade to Le Mans

XKC 030

Chassis number	XKC 030
Distributor	Hoffman, New York, USA
Current owner	Edward Sutherland, USA
Engine number	E-1020-8
Registration mark	n/a
Axle ratio	3.54
Body number	K-1030
Date of dispatch	17 December 1952
Colour, original	Black
Colour, current	Black

XKC 030 history:

- Owner: David Hirsch
- 21 February 1953, MacDill Air Force Base, 6 Hour Race, Hirsch and Bob Gegen, tenth
- 8 March 1953, Sebring, 12 Hour Race, Harry Gray and Bob Gegen, fourth
- Car entered in SCCA (Sports Car Club of America) National Races C-modified class until 1965
- 28 May 1953, Bridgehampton, SCCA National Races, Harry Gray, rolled car, did not finish
- Owner/driver: Loyal Katskee, Nebraska
- Autumn 1953 car advertised for sale $6,000
- 2 May 1954, Iowa City, SCCA National Races, first overall
- 21 June 1954, Chanute Air Force Base, SCCA National Races, second overall, second in class
- 8 August 1954, Lockbourne Air Force Base, SCCA National Races, fifth overall,
- 4 July 1954, Offutt Air Force Base, SCCA National Races, third overall
- 15 August 1954, Milwaukee, SCCA Regional Races, third overall
- (Katskee ranked sixth in Class C-Modified national point standings in 1954)
- 12 March 1955, Sebring, 12 Hour Race, fourth in class
- 30 May 1955, Iowa City, SCCA Regional Races, first overall, Iowa Trophy winner
- 5 September 1955, Kansas City, SCCA National Races, third overall, third in class
- Owner/driver: Herb Hoeffler, Jr.
- 27 May 1956, Thompson, SCCA Regional Races, seventh overall
- 7 July 1956, Beverly, National Championship Races, did not finish
- Owner/driver from 1957 to 1967: Gordon C MacKenzie
- 2 September 1957, Thompson, SCCA National Championship Races, first in class, first race in C-type
- 8 September 1957, Lime Rock, Connecticut Sports Car Club Races, did not finish, mechanical failure
- 20 September 1957, Watkins Glen, SCCA National Championship Races

XKC 030 at Watkins Glen in 1958.
Photo courtesy Corsa Research.

- 6 October 1957, Thompson, New England Region SCCA Races, third in class, car painted white
- 20 October 1957, Thompson, SCCA Regional Races, third overall
- 10 November 1957, Lime Rock, Long Island Sports Car Association Races, second overall, first in class
- 20 April 1958, Marlboro, SCCA President's Cup National Races, fourth overall, fourth in class
- 27 April 1958, Lime Rock, SCCA New England Championship Races, fourth overall, first in class
- 17 May 1958, Lime Rock, Long Island Sports Car Association Races, second overall, second in class
- 25 May 1958, Thompson, SCCA New England Championship Races, fourth overall, fourth in class
- 15 June 1958, Lime Rock, SCCA National Championship Races, tenth overall, third gear only
- 5 July 1958, Lime Rock, SCCA National Championship Races, fourth in class
- 13 July 1958, Lime Rock, Long Island Sports Car Association Races, second in class
- 20 July 1958, Thompson, SCCA New York Championship Races, sixth overall, first in class

XKC 030 cont...

- 27 July 1958, Lime Rock, Westchester Sports Car Club Races, first overall
- 17 August 1958, Montgomery, SCCA National Championship Races, sixth overall, second in class
- 1 September 1958, Thompson, SCCA National Championship Races, fourth overall, third in class
- 14 September 1958, Bridgehampton, SCCA Regional Races, sixth overall, second in class
- 20 September 1958, Watkins Glen, SCCA National Championship Races, fourth overall, fourth in class
- 30 September 1958, Thompson, SCCA Regional Races, third overall, first in class
- 5 October 1958, Thompson, SCCA New England Championship Races, fourth overall, third in class
- 19 October 1958, Lime Rock, SCCA New York Championship Races, fifth in class
- 26 April 1959, Lime Rock, SCCA Regional Races, fifth overall, second in class
- 2 May 1959, Lime Rock, Long Island Sports Car Association Races, first overall
- 9 May 1959, Lime Rock, SCCA Regional Races, fifth overall, second in class
- 23 May 1959, Thompson, SCCA Regional Races, sixth overall, second in class
- 7 June 1959, Vineland, SCCA Regional Races, second overall
- 21 June 1959, Mount Equinox, SCCA hill climb, second overall, first and fastest time of day in class, 4m 48s
- 29 June 1959, Montgomery, acceleration runs, fourth overall
- 7 July 1959, Lime Rock, SCCA National Championship Races, third in class
- 11July 1959, Lime Rock, SCCA Regional Races, fourth overall, first in class
- 19 July 1959, Thompson, SCCA Regional Races, third overall, first in class
- 25 July 1959, Lime Rock, USAC Formula Libre Races, fifteenth overall
- 1 August 1959, Giant's Despair, SCCA hill climb, third overall, third in class
- 10 August 1959, Montgomery, SCCA Airport National Races, fifth in class
- 16 August 1959, Thompson, Long Island Sports Car Association Races, second overall, first in class
- 6 September 1959, Thompson, SCCA National Races, third in class
- 12 September 1959, Lime Rock, Long Island Sports Car Association Races, third overall, first in class
- 26 September 1959, Watkins Glen, SCCA National Championship Races, sixth overall, sixth in class, MacKenzie's 100th race
- 4 October 1959, Thompson, SCCA Regional Races, fifth overall
- 17 October 1959, Lime Rock, SCCA Regional Championship Races, first in class, glasses broke, glass in eye
- 31 October 1959, Lime Rock, SCCA Regional Races, fourth overall, second in class
- 2 April 1960, Lime Rock, MG Car Club Races, fifth overall, car painted green
- 10 April 1960, Vineland, SCCA Regional Races, fourth overall, second in class
- 17 April 1960, Marlboro, SCCA President's Cup National Race, ninth overall, third in class
- 23 April 1960, Lime Rock, SCCA Regional Races, third overall, third in class
- 22 May 1960, Thompson, SCCA Regional Races, fifth overall
- 11 June 1960, Lime Rock, Long Island Sports Car Association Races, third overall, first in class
- 19 June 1960, Roosevelt, Vanderbilt Cup Races, sixth overall, first in class
- 26 June 1960, Mount Equinox, SCCA hill climb, first overall, 4m 46s, fastest time of day
- 2 July 1960, Lime Rock, SCCA National Championship Races, sixth overall, first in class
- 17 July 1960, Thompson, SCCA Regional Races, fifth overall, second in class
- 7 August 1960, Montgomery, SCCA Regional Races, second in class
- 5 September 1960, Thompson, SCCA National Championship Races, eighth overall, third in class
- 10 September 1960, Lime Rock, Long Island Sports Car Association Race, third overall, second in class
- 17 September 1960, Lime Rock, SCCA Regional Races, third overall, first in class
- 24 September 1960, Watkins Glen, SCCA National Championship Races, fourth overall, third in class

long time owner of XKC 030, Gordon MacKenzie (1857-67), here in the mid-1960s; note the D-type like faired headrest
'o Vytal/JDHT

XKC 030 cont...

- 8 October 1960, Thompson, SCCA Regional Races, tenth overall, fourth in class, broken throttle linkage
- 9 October 1960, Thompson, SCCA Regional Races, second in class
- 22 October 1960, Lime Rock, SCCA Regional Race, second overall, first in class
- 12 November 1960, Lime Rock, Long Island Sports Car Association Races, fourth overall, first in class
- 9 April 1961, Vineland, Delaware Valley SCCA Races, second in class
- 22 April 1961, Lime Rock, SCCA Regional Races, seventh overall, third in class
- 21 May 1961, Thompson, SCCA Regional Races, fourth overall, second in class
- 11 June 1961, Vineland, SCCA Divisional Championship Races, eighth overall, second in class
- 18 June 1961, Mount Equinox, SCCA hill climb, second overall, first in class, broke record
- 24 June 1961, Lime Rock, Long Island Sports Car Association Races, fourth overall, third in class
- 1 July 1961, Lime Rock, SCCA Regional Races, sixth overall, second in class
- 4 September 1961, Thompson, SCCA National Races, did not finish, brakes failed, hit banking
- 24 June 1962, Mount Equinox, SCCA hill climb, third overall, second in class, 4m 48s, fog
- 30 June 1962, Lime Rock, SCCA National Races, tenth overall, fifth in class
- 15 July 1962, Thompson, SCCA Northeast Division Races, did not finish, engine smoking
- 21 July 1962, Lime Rock, Long Island Sports Car Association races, withdrew, piston exploded
- 25 August 1962, Lime Rock, SCCA Regional Races, did not finish, more piston problems
- 3 September 1962, Thompson, SCCA National Races, withdrew, blown piston again
- 13 October 1962, Thompson, SCCA Divisional Races, did not start, melted piston
- 20 October 1962, Lime Rock, SCCA Regional Championship Races, withdrew
- 21 April 1963, Vineland, SCCA Divisional Championship Races, seventh overall, second in class
- 4 May 1963, Lime Rock, Long Island Sports Car Association Races, third overall, second in class
- 19 May 1963, Vineland, SCCA Regional Races, third overall, third in class
- 25 May 1963, Thompson, SCCA Regional Races, sixth overall, first in class
- 9 June 1963, Vineland, SCCA Division Championship Races, did not finish, swallowed valve
- 22 June 1963, Mount Equinox, SCCA hill climb, tenth overall, first in class
- 28 September 1963, Lime Rock, SCCA Regional Races, first in class
- 5 October 1963, Lime Rock, Long Island Sports Car Association Races, third overall, first in class
- 13 October 1963, Thompson, SCCA Regional Races, eleventh overall, third in class
- 19 October 1963, Lime Rock, SCCA Regional Championship Races, seventh overall, first in class
- 25 April 1964, Lime Rock, Long Island Sports Car Association Races, first overall
- 2 May 1964, Lime Rock, SCCA Regional Championship Races, seventh overall, second in class
- 24 May 1964, Thompson, SCCA Regional Races, eighth overall, third in class
- 13 June 1964, Lime Rock, SCCA Regional Races, seventh overall, second in class
- 21 June 1964, Thompson, SCCA National Championship Races, fourth overall, second in class
- 28 June 1964, Mount Equinox, SCCA hill climb, second overall, second in class, 4m 34s
- 4 July 1964, Lime Rock, Long Island Sports Car Association. Races, third overall
- 14 August 1964, Lime Rock, SCCA Championship Races, fourth overall, third in class
- 16 August 1964, Thompson, SCCA Regional Championship Races, sixth overall, second in class
- 29 August 1964, Lime Rock, SCCA Championship Races, retired, valve problems
- 19 June 1965, Lime Rock, SCCA Regional Races, fifth overall, first in class
- 26 June 1965, Lime Rock, BSCOA Races, second overall
- 5 July 1965, Lime RCA, SCCA National Races, twelfth overall, fifth in class
- 28 August 1965, Lime Rock, SCCA Regional Races, second overall, fifth in class
- September 6, 1965, Thompson, SCCA National Championship Races, did not start, valve failed
- 1966/67, SCCA National races, C-sports car class entered
- 20 May 1966, Thompson, SCCA Regional Races, fifth overall, fifth in class
- 30 May 1966, Thompson, SCCA Area Championship Races, sixth overall, second in class

XKC 030 cont...

- 11 June 1966, Lime Rock, SCCA Area Championship Races, sixth overall, second in class
- 17 June 1966, Mount Equinox, SCCA hill climb, second overall, second in class, 4m 35s
- 4 July 1966, Lime Rock, SCCA National Championship Races, seventh overall, second in class
- 30 July 1966, Lime Rock, BSCOA & LISCA Inter-Club Races, fifth overall, second in class
- 15 October 1966, Lime Rock, SCCA Area Championship Races, fifth overall, third in class
- 22 April 1967, Lime Rock, SCCA Area 1 Championship Races, third overall, second in class
- 13 May 1967, Lime Rock, SCCA Mohawk-Hudson Regional Races, second overall, second in class
- 28 May 1967, Thompson, SCCA Regional and Area 1 Championships, second overall, second in class
- 4 July 1967, Lime Rock, SCCA National Championship Races, seventh overall, sixth in class
- 26 August 1967, Lime Rock, SCCA Area 1 Championship Races, seventh overall, third in class, rain and fouled plug
- 4 September 1967, Lime Rock, SCCA National Races, sixth overall, fourth in class
- 14 October 1967, Lime Rock, SCCA Area 1 Championship Races, seventh overall, fourth in class, Gordon's last race in the C-type
- Races entered by Gordon MacKenzie in C-type 1957-1967: 84 races; finished first, second, or third in class, in 72% of races
- November 1967, sold to Ed Sutherland, car was not raced from 1968 to 1988. Since 1988 Ed has raced it at several vintage events in the VSCCA (Vintage Sports Car Club of America) over two litre class
- 4 September 1989, Lime Rock, BMW Vintage Fall Festival (1959 Formula Libre Reunion), Gordon MacKenzie
- 6 April 1990, Lime Rock, VSCCA Spring sprints
- 8 July 1990, NHIS Loudon, VSCCA Belknap Cup Races
- 3 September 1990, Lime Rock, BMW Vintage Fall Festival
- 20 October 1990, Lime Rock, VSCCA Fall Finale
- 6 April 1991, Lime Rock, VSCCA Spring sprints
- 27 April 1991, Pocono, VSCCA Races
- 8 June 1991, Mount Equinox, VSCCA hill climb, Malcolm Donaldson Award
- 5 July 1991, NHIS Loudon, VSCCA Belknap Cup Races
- 1 August 1991, Lime Rock, Jaguar Club Races, did not finish, spun. Crankshaft bearing problem
- 19 October 1991, Lime Rock, VSCCA Fall Finale
- 4 April 1992, Lime Rock, VSCCA Spring sprints
- 25 April 25 1992, Pocono, VSCCA Races
- 13 June 1992, Mount Equinox, VSCCA hill climb
- 30 June 1992, NHIS Loudon, VSCCA Belknap Cup Races
- 20 August 1992, Laguna Seca, Monterey Historic Races (Jaguar Featured Marque), Six original C-types racing
- 3 September 1992, Lime Rock, BMW Vintage Fall Festival, Winner Coors Light Cup
- 1 July 1993, NHIS Loudon, VSCCA Belknap Cup Races
- 14 August 1993, Bridgehampton, VSCCA Races
- 2 September 1993, Lime Rock, BMW Vintage Fall Festival
- 11 June 1994, Mount Equinox, VSCCA hill climb
- 1 July 1994, NHIS Loudon, VSCCA DeMoulas Cup Races
- 5 Aug 1994, Lime Rock, VSCCA and Jaguar Club Races
- 1 September 1994, Lime Rock, BMW Vintage Fall Festival
- 10 June 1995, Mount Equinox, VSCCA hill climb, 5min.s 11sec.s
- 17 June 1995, Lime Rock, VSCCA and Jaguar Club Races, did not finish, broke axle half-shaft
- 22 September 1995, Lime Rock, VSCCA Fall Finale
- 7 June 1996, Mount Equinox, VSCCA hill climb, 5min.s 08sec.s
- 14 June 1996, Lime Rock, VSCCA and Jaguar Club Races
- 18 October 1996, Lime Rock, VSCCA Fall Finale
- 29 September 1996, Castle Hill, VSCCA Concours d'Elegance, Winner: Most Significant Post War Car Award
- 6 June 1997, Lime Rock, VSCCA and Jaguar Club Races
- 14 June 1997, Mount Equinox, VSCCA hill climb, 5min.s 07sec.s
- 24 October 1997, Lime Rock, VSCCA Fall Finale
- 5/7June 1998, Lime Rock, VSCCA and Jaguar Club Races
- 13 June 1998, Mount Equinox, VSCCA hill climb, rained out after practice run
- 23 October 1998, Lime Rock, VSCCA Fall Finale

XKC 031

Chassis number	XKC 031
Distributor	Hornburg, Los Angeles, USA
Current owner	Richard Mellen, USA
Engine number	E-1031-8
Registration mark	n/a
Axle ratio	3.54
Body number	K-1031
Date of dispatch	12 January 1953
Colour, original	Silver
Colour, current	British Racing Green

XKC 031 history:

- Supplied to Hornburg, USA
- Supplied by Hornburg to International Motors, Hollywood, California, USA
- Sold to Donald Parkinson
- 19 April 1953, Pebble Beach races California, crashed car, wrecked bonnet. New bonnet ordered, damaged bonnet obtained from 024, repaired and installed
- Early 1954, Torrey Pines races, California, J.M. Jackson, fifth
- 1954, December, for sale by Jackson, with original repaired bonnet from 024 on car (it had the K-1024 body tag on it). Nearby in the same garage was a new red primer bonnet still in its open air factory crate
- 1955, sold to Harrison Evans of Los Angeles, new bonnet installed by Evans, painted Racing Green. Panels from 024 bonnet used for 033 bonnet
- Late 1956 for sale by Evans, sold to Jack Rataree, Arizona.
- 1960, sold to Rich Johnson, Arizona, USA
- 1967, sold to Richard Mellen, USA, now under restoration

The interior and dashboard of XKC 032 today
Photo courtesy Julio Palmaz

Owner/driver Harrison Evans in XKC 031 at Willow Springs, California, 1955
Photo ©JDHT

XKC 032, driven by Ernie Erickson, 1953
Photo courtesy Terry Larson

XKC 032

Chassis number	XKC 032
Distributor	Bourgeois, Belgian Motor Company, Belgium
Current owner	Amalia Palmaz, USA
Engine number	E-1032-8
Registration mark	n/a
Axle ratio	3.54
Body number	K-1032
Date of dispatch	2 January 1953
Colour, original	Birch Grey
Colour, current	Birch Grey

XKC 032 history:

- Supplied to Belgian Motor Company
- Displayed at the 1953 Brussels Motor Show
- Sold to the 1950 Grand Prix world champion, Giuseppe Farina
- Lent to Ferrari for evaluation
- Panhard rod fitted in place of 'A' bracket
- 1953/54, sold to Ernie Erickson, USA; fitted with triple Weber carburettors
- 1954, Abraham Lincoln trophy, Washington DC, second or third
- Chanute, Illinois, second
- 1955, sold to 'Doc' Wyllie, who previously owned XKC 009
- Seneca Cup, Watkins Glen; first
- November, Fairchild Airport, Maryland, second in class
- 1957, September, sold to J P Jefferson Scott, fitted with S.U. carburettors once again; owned and used by him until 1980
- During Scott's ownership, the car was fitted with a Ford 4.7 V8 engine and Borg Warner all synchromesh gearbox
- The Jaguar engine and gearbox were later refitted
- Passed through Dan Margulies, London
- 1983, sold to Pat Burke, Sydney, Australia
- 1984, August, driven by Stirling Moss and Warwick Brown at Amaroo Park, Sydney
- Substantial restoration by John Pearson UK
- Owned by Kerry Manolas, Australia
- 1990, auctioned by Brooks at Monaco and reported sold for £868,000 to Boris Messmer, Germany
- 1994, sold through Gregor Fisken to Julio and Amalia Palmaz, USA

Believed to be Giuseppe Farina in XKC 032, in the garage of the Belgian Motor Company in 1953
Photo ©JDHT

XKC 032, by owner Dr Julio C Palmaz

We bought the car unseen from Gregor Fisken from London. All his representations of the car turned out to be correct and accurate. Later I found out that the car had last been restored by John Pearson, this was long after John finished a D-type restoration for me! Actually, I have never entered XKC 032 in a race, but I look forward to participate with it in the C-type reunion in 2001, on the occasion of the fiftieth anniversary of the first Jaguar victory at Le Mans.

I have not driven any other C-type except mine. Compared to my D-type, it is very sedate and docile at low speeds. Yet, its performance above 4000 rpm is surprisingly strong and lively.

The brakes are fairly powerful, and the cornering positive and sharp. The car behaves much like other live rear axle, front engined sports cars of the early fifties, by swinging the tail out if pushed. On a scale of agility, I rank the C-type above the Aston Martin DB3S, Allard J2, Frazer-Nash Le Mans replica and Maserati A6CGS, and below the Jaguar D-type and the Lister 'knobbly'. We are fortunate to own all these cars, so I can compare them side by side – and I frequently do.

XKC 033

Chassis number	XKC 033
Distributor	Hornburg, Los Angeles, USA
Current owner	Walter Hill, USA
Engine number	E-1033-8
Registration mark	n/a
Axle ratio	3.73
Body number	K-1033
Date of dispatch	28 November 1952
Colour, original	British Racing Green with Silver interior trim
Colour, current	British Racing Green with Light Green interior trim

XKC

XKC 033 history:

- Supplied to Hornburg, USA
- Sold to Mr McManus
- 4 July 1953, Offutt Air Force Base, Nebraska, second race Robert McManus, sixth; fourth race Chuck Hassen, fourth
- 27 September 1953, Stout Field Races, Indianapolis, main event, Chuck Hassen, retired 33rd lap, worn tyres and transmission problems
- 1953 fall meeting at Mansfield, Louisiana; 1953 fall meeting and 1954 spring meeting Eagle Mountain Lake, Texas, at all three meetings first in class and second overall
- 1954, sold to Riddelle Gregory (Masten's brother) who installed a Le Mans head, 40mm Weber carburettors and latest rear suspension. Car repainted light grey
- 28 March 1954, Bergstrom Air Force Base, Texas, second race, Riddelle Gregory, second overall and in class
- 11 April 1954, Pebble Beach Races, California, Riddelle Gregory, third overall, second in class
- 1954 fall meeting Eagle Mountain Lake first; at Golden Gate crashed in practice, leaked oil in race and black flagged; Albany, Georgia, and Savannah, Georgia, at both events blew engine in practice; Mansfield, second overall, first in class
- 1954, late summer, Fort Worth SCCA Races, Texas, main event, Riddelle Gregory retired, threw rod through block and aluminium sump
- Used block installed
- Late 1954, sold to Tom Groskritz who purchased new aluminium sump
- Paint stripped off and repainted racing green, seats redone in tan naugahyde
- 10 July 1955, Torrey Pines Races, California, retired when running fourth overall, lost oil pressure
- 1955, Pomona Races, California, practiced only, too much rain on Sunday
- 12 November 1955, Grand Central Races, Glendale, California, practised only, mechanical problems
- 4 November 1956, Palm Springs Races, California, retired, car overheated
- 18 November 1956,Paramount Ranch Races California, main event, eighth overall, second in class
- 10 March 1957, Paramount Ranch Races, main event, lost it on uphill turn, blinded by sun, crunched bonnet; new front sub frame, new grille, new bonnet built, using panels from 024 bonnet with K 1024 tag; 40mm Webers removed, 2 inch S.U. carburettors fitted
- 1958, car sold to Robert Lane California
- Car sold to Stuart McCallum California
- June 1968, car advertised for sale by McCallum in *Road and Track*, disassembled
- Later owned by George Boyd; car badly damaged when tornado collapsed building
- 1970's, sold to Walter C Hill, USA, restored to XKC 003 specifications

Tom Groskritz in XKC 033 at Palm Springs, 4 November 1956.
Photo courtesy Tom Groskritz.

XKC 034

Chassis number	XKC 034
Distributor	Hoffman, New York, USA
Current owner	Tom Jaycox, USA
Engine number	E-1036-8
Registration mark	n/a
Axle ratio	3.31
Body number	K-1034
Date of dispatch	23 January 1953
Colour, original	British Racing Green
Colour, current	Not known

XKC 034 history:

- Supplied to Hoffman, USA
- Sold to Jack Shepherd, Tampa, Florida, USA
- 1953, March, Sebring 12 Hour Race, driven by George Huntoon/Phil Stiles
- 25 October 1953, Turner Air Force Base, Albany, Georgia, first race, George Huntoon
- 31 January 1954, Mac Dill Air Force Base, Tampa, Florida, George Huntoon, second race, fifth; main event fifth; still in British Racing Green, original cloth seats
- 1954, sold to Lorin McMullen, Fort Worth, Texas
- 1954, late summer, Fort Worth Races, Texas, SCCA Regional Race, Lorin McMullen, second race third, fifth race second
- 5 September 1955, Fairfax Races, Missouri, Lorin McMullen third race, twelfth
- Later sold in heavily damaged state and fitted with V8 power unit
- Sold to Bill Zorn, Illinois
- Sold to Dave Rubin, owner of XKC 022, of New York, Zorn kept V8 engine, original gearbox was badly damaged
- 1964, sold to Mark Daniels, Milwaukee, Wisconsin, USA
- Sold to Jim Grief, Wisconsin
- Sold to Ali Lugo
- Some parts had been fitted to XKC 015
- Purchased in 1975 by Tom Jaycox, USA
- 1996, long term restoration completed

XKC 035

Chassis number	XKC 035
Distributor	Delecroix, Paris, France
Current owner	Allen Lloyd, GB
Engine number	E-1037-8
Registration mark	WWK 4
Axle ratio	3.31
Body number	K-1035
Date of dispatch	15 January 1953
Colour, original	Birch Grey
Colour, current	British Racing Green with Green interior trim

XKC 035 history:

- Supplied to Delecroix, Paris, France
- Sold to Henri Peignaux, Lyons
- Sold to Jean Heaurtaux
- 1953, Soleil-Cannes Rally
- Mille Miglia, accompanied by Madame Heaurtaux as co-driver, Captain Crespin failed to arrive in time, completed course but not placed
- Planfoy hill climb, St Etienne, broke record but Heaurtaux crashed after the finish and was killed
- Many years later, remains found in France and returned to the UK
- Owned at some time by John Harper
- Owned by Phil Bennett who rebuilt and re-registered the car WWK 4 in the early 1980's
- Sold to Jeffrey Pattinson
- Bought at auction in the late 1980's by Allen Lloyd UK
- 1991 and 1993, Jaguar factory cavalcades to Le Mans

XKC 036

Madame Berthomier in XKC 036 with local fans in Dakar after the 1953 race
Photo ©JDHT

Chassis number	XKC 036
Distributor	Moto Maroc, Casablanca
Current owner	Bill Marriot, USA
Engine number	E-1034-8
Registration mark	OLT 393
Axle ratio	3.31
Body number	K-1036
Date of dispatch	12 January 1953
Colour, original	Cream
Colour, current	Red

XKC 036 history:

- Supplied to Moto Maroc, Casablanca, Morocco
- 1953, Sold to Guy Berthomier, Casablanca
- 1953, Dakar Grand Prix, first, over 2 litre class
- 1953, Marrakesh Grand Prix, fourth
- 1953, Portuguese Grand Prix meeting, Oporto, crashed
- 1953, August, factory quoted £53 for a new chassis and £315 for a new body
- Owned by C. Bavery, France for many years
- Sold to Philippe Renault
- Sold, via Adrian Hamilton, to Matt Spitzley, Oxfordshire, UK
- 1991 and 1993, Jaguar factory cavalcade to Le Mans
- Restored with a 3.8 litre engine and 45DCO3 Weber carburettors and disc brakes
- 1997, sold to Bill Marriot, USA

Guy Berthomier, owner/driver ofXKC 036, after winning his class in the Dakar Grand Prix in 1953
Photo ©JDHT

XKC 037

Chassis number	XKC 037
Distributor	n/a
Current owner	Greg Johnson, USA
Engine number	E-1038-8
Registration mark	NDU 970, now HV22J2
Axle ratio	3.31
Body number	K-1037
Date of dispatch	9 January 1953
Colour, original	Dark Green
Colour, current	British Racing Green with Green interior Trim

XKC 037 works car history:

- Built as production car, but taken over by Experimental Department, completed 20 April 1953
- 1953, reserve Le Mans car and used by Experimental Department
- 1953, Silverstone, International Meeting, Jaguar 'works' entry, Stirling Moss, car number 35. Moss rolled car in practice, it was rebuilt overnight at factory (cylinder head W.266, gearbox number JH.13310, 4.09 axle, Lockheed twin leading shoe brakes, Champion NA-10 plugs), placed seventh
- 1953, June, Le Mans, 'works' preparation for Jaguar factory entry but not raced
- 1953, September, sold as home delivery export car via Lewis and Hodgkiss, Kenya to John Manussis, Kenya
- Repainted Birch Grey with blue wheels and Kenyan emblem on both flanks
- 1953, September, Dundrod time trials, C J Manussis, car number 14, crashed, rebuilt at factory again, reportedly with new body and chassis
- Owner wanted car prepared for 1954 Le Mans but problems with insurance company over repair costs prevented this
- 1954, Goodwood Whitsunday Meet, Gerry Dunham Jr., Weber carburettors fitted, third place
- 1954, April, Oulton Park, British Empire Trophy Race, Gerry Dunham Jr.
- 1954, May, Aintree, Gerry Dunham Jr., car number 75
- 1954, June, Goodwood, Gerry Dunham Jr., car number 28
- 1954, July, Silverstone British Grand Prix Meeting, C J Manussis, car number 38
- 1954, July, Reims 12 Hour, C J Manussis and Gerry Dunham Jr., car number 4, retired
- 1954, exported as a legal requirement within one year of purchase, to Australia
- 1954, August, sold via Peter Whitehead to Dr John Boorman, Cessnock, New South Wales
- Used as road and race car with a mixture of successes and accidents, including two large accidents
- Gnoo Blass Sports Car Championship, John Boorman
- Mount Panorama, 8 Hours Day Weekend, John Boorman
- 1955, April, Bathurst 100 Meet, John Boorman
- 1955, October, Bathurst Motor Races, John Boorman
- 1955, October, Orange Motor Races, John Boorman
- 1956, sold to Frank Gardner where the engine, steering and exhaust system were reputed to have been fitted temporarily to Gardner's racing XK120 (660162)
- Car was rebuilt, with original repaired body and 18 gauge alloy bonnet, engine, steering etc. Chassis repaired by Gardner and some mechanical parts flown in from U.K, bonnet shape altered and fitted first with XK120 grille, then Allard J2 grille
- 1957, March, Mount Druitt Races, Frank Gardner, first
- 1957, April, Bathurst 100 Meet, Frank Gardner
- 1957, May, Mount Druitt Motor Races, Frank Gardner

XKC 037, driven by Stirling Moss as a 'works' entry, Silverstone International Meeting, 1953
Photo courtesy Greg Johnson

XKC 037 cont...

- 1957, June, Mount Druitt Motor Races, Frank Gardner
- 1957, June, Lowood Motor Races, Frank Gardner
- 1957, July, Mount Druitt Sprints, Frank Gardner
- 1957, August, Mount Druitt Motor Races, Frank Gardner
- 1957, September, Silverdale hill climb, Frank Gardner
- 1957, October, Bathurst Road Racing, Frank Gardner, second
- 1957, October, Foley's Hill hill climb, Frank Gardner
- 1957, November, Mount Druitt Races, Frank Gardner
- 1957, several successes and car was unbeaten at the sports car scratch races at Mount Druitt and Bathurst, nearly winning the ARDC championship
- 1958, June, Orange Races, Frank Gardner
- 1958, June, Foley's Hill hill climb, Frank Gardner
- 1958, October, sold to Frank Matich of Leaton Motors, raced by Matich, recorded 146.34 mph at Bathurst
- 1958, October, Silverdale hill climb, Frank Matich
- 1959, January, Orange Fifth Pacific Road Race Championship, Matich
- 1959, March, Bathurst 100 Meeting, Frank Matich
- 1959, April, Lowood Saloon Car Championship, Frank Matich
- 1959, June, Lowood Trophy Races, Frank Matich
- 1959, August, Lowood Motor Races, Ross Dalton
- 1959, October, Orange Motor Races, Ross Dalton
- 1959, October, Lowood Motor Races, Ross Dalton
- 1960, February, Orange Motor Races, Ross Dalton
- 1960, June, Huntley Colliery hill climb, Ross Dalton
- 1960, June, Hume Weir Motor Races, Ross Dalton
- 1961, January, Warwick Farm Races, Ross Dalton
- 1961, restored to more original appearance, XK150 disc brakes fitted
- 1963, November, Towac, T Watts
- 1964, March, sold to John Kinsella, Sydney, Australia, with blown block which was replaced with a 3.8-litre E-type block
- 1966, sold to Peter Lonergan, Queensland
- 1969, sold to Ian Cummins
- 1970, commenced 5 year restoration
- 1976, Silverdale hill climb, crashed and rebuilt again
- 1977, sold to George Parlby, Sydney, Australia, for Aus$40.000
- Sold to Toyshop, New South Wales
- Sold to USA for a reported $102,000
- 1986, sold to Eric Traber, Switzerland
- 1993, sold to Greg Johnson, USA
- 1995, restored and prepared for vintage racing by Terry Larson, Arizona, USA
- 1996, August, Monterey Historic Automobile races
- 1997, March, HMSA Spring event; May, Wine Country Classic; August, Monterey Pre-Historic Automobile races and Historic Automobile races; November, Chrysler Speed Festival at Coronado Island Naval Air Station
- 1998, March, HMSA Spring Event race; August, Monterey Pre-Historic Automobile races and Historic Automobile races; November, Chrysler Speed Festival at Coronado Island Air Station
- 1999, March, HMSA Spring Event race; August, Monterey Pre-Historic Automobile races and Historic Automobile races; October, Chrysler Speed Festival at Coronado Naval Air Station
- 2000, March, HMSA Spring Event races; May, Wine Country Classic race; August, Monterey Pre-Historic Automobile races and Historic Automobile race; November, Chrysler Speed Festival at Coronado Naval Air Station
- Still owned by Greg Johnson, USA

XKC 037 driven by Dr John Boorman at Bathurst, Australia, 1955
Photo courtesy Terry McGrath

Duncan Hamilton bought XKC 038 in 1954, here he is winning at Aintree later that year
Photo Klemantaski/JDHT

XKC 038

Chassis number	XKC 038
Distributor	n/a
Current owner	Sir Anthony Bamford, UK
Engine number	E-1038-8, then E-1052-8
Registration mark	OVC 915 (original)
Axle ratio	3.92
Body number	K-1038
Date of dispatch	4 April 1954
Colour, original	Dark Green
Colour, current	Suede Green

XKC 038 works car history:

- 1953, works car, Le Mans, was practice car for Norman Dewis (number 18 and fitted with drum brakes)
- After race, car was built up to full 1953 'works' specification, except for petrol tank and light construction; air scoop added to bonnet
- Prepared for Mexican Road Race but never raced
- 1954, displayed at Geneva Motor Show
- Sold to Duncan Hamilton
- British Empire Trophy, Oulton Park, first in heat, fourth in handicap final and first on road
- Members' Meeting at Goodwood, second; Aintree first; Montlhéry first
- Sold to Dan Margulies
- Raced extensively in the UK and overseas by the owner and once by his mechanic, Graham Hill
- 1955, Castle Combe first, Sardinia fourth
- 1956, Targa Florio with David Piper, sixteenth, delayed by crash
- Sold to Gillie Tyrer
- 1957, sold to Peter Mould
- 1958, sold to Peter Sargent
- Later owners included Tom Gibson, Frank Sowden, Rupert Glydon, Michael Hall, and Ralph Stross, Cheshire; also advertised in *Road and Track*, February 1967, by Dudley B Gates, Bayville, New York, USA
- 1991, Jaguar factory cavalcade to Le Mans
- 1995, restoration by John Pearson
- Owned by Sir Anthony Bamford, UK

XKC 039

Chassis number	XKC 039
Distributor	Henlys, London, UK
Current owner	Steffan Svenby, Sweden
Engine number	E-1040-8
Registration mark	RKX 991 (original)
Axle ratio	3.92
Body number	K-1039
Date of dispatch	21 April 1953
Colour, original	British Racing Green with Silver interior Trim
Colour, current	British Racing Green

XKC 039 history:

- Supplied to Henlys, though effectively a direct sale to Peter Whitehead
- 1953, Goodwood, Graham Whitehead driving, first
- Silverstone International, Graham Whitehead, sixth
- Hyères 12 Hours, driven by owner and Tom Cole, first
- Lisbon, with Pescara and Hamilton retired, sixth
- 1954, January, Mount Druitt, Australia with Tony Gaze and Alf Barrett, retired after leading
- Taken by owner to New Zealand
- Sold to Jack Tutton, New Zealand, president of Canterbury Car Club
- C. W. F. Hamilton Trophy, Christchurch, fifth (provisional as Tutton protested that he was baulked by fourth place 498cc Cooper Norton)
- 1957, sold to Des Wilde
- Soon sold to David Young
- Known to have been raced from November to January 1961
- Sold to Garth Forsythe
- 1966, sold to Ian and Ray Archibald, South Island Jaguar distributors, raced in historic events
- 1988, sold to Peter Agg, UK
- 1991, Jaguar factory cavalcade to Le Mans
- 1995, sold to Francesco Scianna, Italy
- 1997, sold to Steffan Svenby, Sweden, and 'race prepared' by Don Law, England
- 2000, raced by Justin Law in BRDC 50s Sports Car Championship. First at Silverstone, Brands Hatch and Imola, third overall in Championship
- Goodwood Revival Meeting, first on road, second overall
- Ennstal Classic with Stirling Moss and Dr Wolfgang Reitzle, chairman of Jaguar
- Tour de France, Steffan Svenby and Don Law
- Special features: body work behind drivers seat modified to allow more driver's space

This is XKC 039 during its time in New Zealand, being raced by Ian Archibald sometime in the 1970s
Photo Marshall/JDHT

XKC 040

Chassis number	XKC 040
Distributor	Byatts, Fenton, Stoke-on-Trent, UK
Current owner	Walter Hill, USA
Engine number	E-1035-8
Registration mark	SEH 721 (original)
Axle ratio	3.73
Body number	K-1040
Date of dispatch	10 March 1953
Colour, original	British Racing Green with Silver interior trim
Colour, current	Off-White with Biscuit interior Trim

XKC 040 history:

- Sold to Jim Swift, Director of Byatts, Fenton, Stoke-on-Trent
- Club raced with some success
- Various later UK owners, including Rt Hon C St Aubyn
- 1960, sold by Chequered Flag, London, to Bill Dunn, Florida, USA
- 1980, sold to Walter Hill and restoration began
- Currently owned by Walter Hill, USA

Ian (?) Swift racing XKC 040 in the Isle of Man in 1953
Photo Klemantaski/JDHT

XKC 041

Chassis number	XKC 041
Distributor	Rossleigh, Edinburgh, UK
Current owner	Gregor Fisken family, UK
Engine number	E-1041-8
Registration mark	KSF 181 (Original)
Axle ratio	3.92
Body number	K-1041
Date of dispatch	24 March 1953
Colour, original	Metallic Blue with Silver interior trim
Colour, current	Metallic Blue with Silver interior trim

XKC 041 history:

- Sold to Merchiston Motors, the Ecurie Ecosse base
- 1953, driven by Jimmy Stewart: Charterhall, second; Ibsley, third; Castle Combe; Silverstone, twelfth; Charterhall third; Thruxton, two first places; Snetterton, two third places; Empire Trophy, Isle of Man, fifth in heat, sixth in final; Snetterton, crashed; Silverstone Grand Prix Meeting, sixth; Thruxton, first
- Charterhall, Ian Stewart second
- Goodwood Nine Hours, Ian Stewart/Bob Dickson, fourth
- Nürburgring 1000 kms race, Ian Stewart/Roy Salvadori, second
- 1954, July, sold to Sir James Walker, Berkshire, who retained car for several years
- 1956, new gearbox fitted by works
- Several later owners in the north of England
- 1963, owned by M N Slater later of Golden Fleece Enterprises, Yorkshire; also owned by John Pearson
- 1969, offered for sale by Brian Classic, Didsbury, Manchester
- March 1970, advertised for sale in *Road and Track*, by Brian Classic (chassis number quoted as XKC 041 but car advertised may have been XKC 049, see the history of this car)
- August 1970, advertised for sale in *Motor Sport*, by Christopher Renwick, London W12
- 1971, sold to Gavin Sandford-Morgan, Australia and displayed in Birdwood Motor Museum from 1972
- 1976, sold to John Blanden, Australia
- Occasionally raced by his son Richard
- 1982, February, driven at Sandown 'Tribute to the Champions' meeting by Stirling Moss and Alan Jones
- 2000, sold to the Fisken family, UK
- 2000, Goodwood Revival meeting, Gregor Fisken qualified the car on pole position (in the wet) but finished ninth, as the car was 'set up' for road use

XKC 042

Chassis number	XKC 042
Distributor	Rossleigh, Edinburgh, UK
Current owner	Dick Skipworth, UK
Engine number	E-1042-8
Registration mark	KSF 182 (original)
Axle ratio	3.92
Body number	K-1042
Date of dispatch	2 April 1953
Colour, original	Metallic Blue with Silver interior trim
Colour, current	Metallic Blue with Silver interior trim

XKC

XKC 042 history:

- Originally intended for export to Carlos Lostalo, Argentina, but allegedly cancelled due to customs difficulties. Supplied to Rossleigh, Edinburgh, and sold to Ecurie Ecosse
- 1953, Charterhall, Sanderson fourth and Lawrence, unplaced
- Ibsley, Scott-Douglas, fourth
- Charterhall, Sanderson, second
- Thruxton, Scott-Douglas
- Snetterton, Lawrence, unplaced
- Empire Trophy, Isle of Man, Sanderson, fourth in heat, fifth in final
- Snetterton, Lawrence second and third
- Silverstone Grand Prix Meeting, Sanderson, eleventh
- Thruxton, Lawrence, third
- Charterhall, Jimmy Stewart, third
- Goodwood, Sanderson/Dixon
- Goodwood Nine Hours, Lawrence/Curtis, fifth
- Nürburgring 1000 kms, Jimmy Stewart/Lawrence, sixth
- 1954, sold to John Keeling and raced with some success
- 1954, Zandvort, Robin Carnegie was hit from behind, while running second, by Hans David
- Paris Cup, Montlhéry, crashed
- 1955, Ibsley, Carnegie driving enthusiastically, went off, clearing the straw bales and rolling end over end three times, before finishing upside down
- Later owners included a Mr Elkins and Nigel Dawes, UK, from the early 1970's; also Tony Charnock, Paul Vestey
- Car driven, and impressions published by Philip Porter and Paul Skilleter during Dawes's ownership
- 1983, sold to Peter Alpar, Australia
- 1986, sold via Adrian Hamilton to Campbell McLaren, Scotland
- 1988 and 1989 Mille Miglia, 1991 Jaguar factory cavalcade to Le Mans tour, Campbell McLaren
- 1993, sold to Dick Skipworth, UK, joining the rest of his Ecurie Ecosse collection
- 1993, Mille Miglia and Jaguar factory cavalcade to Le Mans tour
- 1994, Ecurie Ecosse tour
- 1995, Mille Miglia, Goodwood Festival and Italia Classica
- 1996, Ecurie Ecosse tour, Le Mans tour with Tom Candlish, Copenhagen Classic
- 1997, Monte Carlo Historique with Barrie (Whizzo) Williams, Ecurie Ecosse tour
- 1998, Danish tour, Goodwood Revival meeting
- 2000, Goodwood Revival meeting

XKC 042 was bought by Ecurie Ecosse when new. This photo may be at the 1953 Silverstone Grand Prix meeting
Photo ©JDHT

XKC 042, by owner Dick Skipworth

*'Oh how I never wish to see
Another Jaguar in a tree'*

I believe there may be some more lines, but I do not have them on record. This little ditty was coined whist extracting XKC 042 from a tree at Zandvort in 1954. Driven then by Robin Carnegie (now the Earl of Northesk), whilst running second with a real chance of a win, XKC 042 was hit from behind by one of the Ecurie Ecosse ex-works cars, driven by Hans David a lap down. Robin's mechanic was so annoyed that he went to the Ecurie Ecosse pit, and picked a fight with 'Wilkie' Wilkinson.

This was the second time that XKC 042 had been in the bushes, the previous time was at Montlhéry with owner-driver John Keeling. The serious competition career of XKC 042 effectively ended at Ibsley in 1955. Driven enthusiastically by Robin Carnegie, the car went off, cleared the straw bales, and completed three end over end somersaults, before finishing upside down. Robin was fortunately thrown out of the car. Apart from bodywork, there was apparently little damage, but it looked bad enough to convince the insurance company to pay out £1900 as a near write-off.

I was first introduced to XKC 042 in 1991. Campbell McLaren drove me from Glasgow to Troon where I was to join our trimaran for a trip back to the Hamble. Some eighteen months later I was able to buy her (more like a second marriage than a purchase). Since that time she has competed in numerous events, completed numerous tours, and has been driven by such celebrities as Stirling Moss, Tony Brooks and Barrie ('Whizzo') Williams. I suppose that I have come to regard her as the second lady in my life, always responsive, impeccably mannered, exciting when provoked, gracious lines, totally reliable, not too expensive to maintain, well mannered in traffic but prefers the open road, and holds her own in younger company. In fact, I guess there is not much wrong with either...

XKC 043 being campaigned by present owner Aubrey Finburgh
Photo courtesy Aubrey Finburgh

XKC 043

Chassis number	XKC 043
Distributor	Lagerwijs, The Hague, Holland
Current owner	Aubrey Finburgh, UK
Engine number	E-1044-8
Registration mark	PUR 120 (original)
Axle ratio	3.92
Body number	K-1043
Date of dispatch	4 June 1953
Colour, original	British Racing Green
Colour, current	British Racing Green

XKC

XKC 043 history:

- Sold to R E L M Tielens, Meerssen, near Maastricht
- Raced, but not successfully
- 1959/1960 sold to Hans van der Ham, Heelerheide, near Maastricht
- Raced more extensively, including many appearances at Zandvoort, many mid-field finishes
- Early 1960s made last appearance at hill climb near Vaals
- Disappeared from scene
- At some stage sold to Oscar Chiararia
- 1968, found by Peter Zwakman's partner while looking for an XK in South of Holland. Car was spotted in a meadow without engine, gearbox and wheels, used by owner's children to play on. Most missing parts found stored in owner's garage, including the manifold with triple Weber carburettors
- Sold to Zwakman and partner; advertised (by them?) for sale in *Motor Sport* in October 1969
- 1970, sold to XK specialist Aubrey Finburgh; totally restored at Finburgh's Classic Auto Company, completed in 1991
- Raced by Aubrey in the UK, Europe and Laguna Seca. Competed in Tour Auto and Italia Classica, also Le Mans cavalcade. 1998 first Goodwood Revival Meeting, driven by Vanessa Finburgh (Aubrey's daughter) in the Freddie March Memorial Trophy Race. Now raced by Aubrey's son-in-law Flavien Marcais who gained pole position, first in class and third over all in 2000 Historic Grand Prix at Monaco
- Still owned by Aubrey Finburgh, UK

PUR 120

XKC 044

Chassis number	XKC 044
Distributor	Fredlunds, Stockholm, Sweden
Current owner	John Pentis, Australia/USA
Engine number	E-1043-8
Registration mark	17V4
Axle ratio	3.92
Body number	K-1044
Date OF dispatch	1 September 1953
Colour, original	Black
Colour, current	British Racing Green with Green interior trim

XKC

XKC 044 history:

- Sold to Oscar Swahn
- Some local successes
- Sold to Arne Fredlund, son of importer
- 1954, Skarpnäck, Stockholm, second
- Sold to Curt Lincoln
- 1955, Djurgaard, Helsinki, first and second
- Kingsland Trophy
- Brands Hatch, third
- Late 1950's owners included Folke Strid, Hagersten and Tore Bjurstrom
- Sold to Fredlund again
- Being restored until Fredlund Sr. died
- Sold to Eric Magnus Alvan
- Later 1960s imported to UK by Nigel Moores
- May 1970, advertised for sale in *Motor Sport*
- Sold to Robert Harrison, USA
- Sold to Kiichi Harvyyama
- Sold to Yoshiyuki Hayashi, Japan
- 1991, restored by John Pearson, UK, and sold to Sam Mann, USA
- 1996, sold to John Pentis, Australia, but car kept in USA

XKC 045

Chassis number	XKC 045
Distributor	Compagnia Generale Auto, Milan, Italy
Current owner	Jaguar Daimler Heritage Trust, UK
Engine number	E-1046-8
Registration mark	NDU 289 (original)
Axle ratio	3.92
Body number	K-1045
Date of dispatch	10 April 1953
Colour, original	Red with Silver interior trim
Colour, current	British Racing Green

XKC 045 history:

- Sold to Mario Tadini
- 1953, Mille Miglia, with Franco Cortese, retired
- Returned to factory for work
- Sold to Ivo Badaracco, Switzerland
- 1954, Swiss Grand Prix Meeting, third in over 1.6 litre sports car class
- Sold to Silvio Moser, Switzerland, used mainly for hill climbs
- Sold to Hans Maag, used mainly in hill climbs in 1960's
- Sold to Sir Anthony Bamford.
- Sold to Richard L Hubbard.
- Sold to W T Aken and Company, Nigel Bradshaw, St Anne's, Lancashire, UK
- Advertised for sale in *Motor Sport*, September 1970, by David Mulvaney at Brian Classic's in Manchester
- Sold to Bob Roberts, former owner of Midland Motor Museum, Bridgnorth, UK
- Raced occasionally for Roberts by Mike Barker
- Sold to Jaguar Daimler Heritage Trust, Coventry, UK; around this time fitted with a new reproduction bonnet
- 1993, Jaguar factory cavalcade to Le Mans
- 2000, original bonnet acquired by the JDHT
- 2000, Enstal Klassik Rennen, Austria, driven by Stirling Moss and Dr Wolfgang Reitzle

Opposite Page Top:
Fredlund crashed XKC 044 at Hedemora in Sweden in 1954 *Photo ©JDHT*
Bottom:
Oscar Swahn driving XKC 044 at Skarpnack in Sweden in 1953 *Photo ©JDHT*
Above:
The then owner of XKC 045, Hans Maag, in a Swiss hillclimb around 1965 *Photo ©JDHT*

The unique 'reverse flow' SU carburettors on XKC 046
Photo courtesy Tom Candlish

XKC 046

Chassis number	XKC 046
Distributor	Delecroix, Paris, France
Current owner	Tony Wang, USA
Engine number	E-1048-8
Registration mark	MVC 360 (original)
Axle ratio	3.92
Body number	K1046
Date of dispatch	9 April 1953
Colour, original	Metallic Blue
Colour, current	Metallic Blue

XKC 046 history:

- Sold to Sir James Scott-Douglas and used as Ecurie Ecosse team car, and at some time fitted by Wilkie Wilkinson with 'reverse flow' S.U. carburettors, facing the engine, to increase the length of the induction pipes (see photo)
- 1953 Castle Combe, first
- Reims 12 Hours, with Sanderson, fourth
- Spa 24 Hours, with Gale, second
- Nürburgring 1000 kms, crashed in practice, rebuilt
- Sold to Berwyn Baxter, 1954/1955 used successfully in club racing
- 1955, sold to Max Trimble and successfully club raced
- Sold to Lord Ebury
- 1957, fatal accident at Prescott hill climb
- Later owners included John Houghton, who used it on the road
- Sold to Tom May who spent 15 years restoring car
- Late 1970s sold to Tony Hilderbrand
- Early 1980s sold to Lord Anthony Rufus-Izaacs
- Mid 1980s sold via Adrian Hamilton to Tony Wang, USA
- 1992, Monterey historic C- type race

Max Trimble driving XKC 046 at Silverstone, 11 August 1956
Photo ©JDHT

Swaters, flanked by co-driver Laurent and 'Lofty' England, during night-time practice for the 1954 Le Mans
Photo Vachon/JDHT

XKC 047

Chassis number	XKC 047
Distributor	Bourgeois, Belgian Motor Company, Belgium
Current owner	Parts used on XKC 012
Engine number	E-1047-8
Registration mark	N/A
Axle ratio	3.54
Body number	K-1047
Date of dispatch	May 1953
Colour, original	Yellow with Silver interior trim
Colour, current	n/a

XKC 047 works car history:

- Originally intended for Ian Appleyard to rally in 1953
- Sold to Roger Laurent, Belgium
- 1953, prepared by factory for Le Mans as Ecurie Francorchamps entry
- Le Mans, with De Tornaco, ninth
- Spa 24 Hours, with cylinder head number 1047, 3.31:1 axle, retired
- Nürburgring, with Olivier Gendebien, retired
- 1954, crashed by Frank Rainbow and Les Bottrill en route to Le Mans
- XKC 012 sent out to Le Mans and fitted with engine and other parts from 047
- Completed car became known as XKC 047
- Remains of the original 047 trucked back to the factory
- 1954, Le Mans, with Swaters, fourth
- 1954, Reims 12 Hours, with Swaters, finished third behind the two works D-types
- Sold to Walter Arnold, Germany, who was placed seventh in the Barcelona Cup, Barcelona, Spain
- Early 1956, Wolfgang von Trips considered purchasing car but decided against it
- 1954, sold to Lt Col James Gallagher, who was stationed in Germany, in the U.S. Air Force; he was transferred for a tour of duty to Denison, Texas and shipped the C-type with him
- Now owned by Tom Groskritz, USA, but see XKC 012

Laurent and de Tornaco finished ninth in XKC 047 in the 1956 3 Le Mans. The car was yellow, the Belgian racing colour
Photo Pike/JDHT

XKC 048

Chassis number	XKC 048
Distributor	Henlys, London, UK
Current owner	Stanislaus Graf von Donhoff, Germany
Engine number	E-1045-8
Registration mark	OHP 43 (original)
Axle ratio	3.92
Body number	K-1048
Date of dispatch	14 October 1953
Colour, original	French Blue
Colour, current	British Racing Green

XKC 048 in action at recent German event
Photo courtesy Stanislaus Donhoff

XKC 048 history:

- Supplied to Henlys, London, UK
- Sold to Colonel Ronnie Hoare, who used it as a road car abroad and in the UK
- 1956, sold to Michael Crowley-Milling who had a slight incident and extensively damaged the bonnet
- New bonnet purchased at the factory and car painted dark green, fitted different windscreen, all weather equipment and used as a road car
- Later displayed at former Stratford Motor Museum
- 1986, sold to Stanislaus Graf von Donhoff, Germany, put back to original and used in club racing, including 1988 Mille Miglia.

XKC 049

Chassis number	XKC 049
Distributor	Truman, Nottingham, UK
Current owner	Aba Kogan, Canada
Engine number	E-1050-8
Registration mark	RAU 450 (original)
Axle ratio	3.92
Body number	K-1049
Date of dispatch	16 July 1953
Colour, original	British Racing Green with Silver interior trim
Colour, current	British Racing Green

XKC 049 history:

- Used in club racing by Don Truman
- 1955, sold to Gillie Tyrer who fitted XK 120 Roadster windscreen and hood
- Sold to Louis Manduca
- Unlimited Sports Car Race, Brands Hatch, Archie Scott-Brown, first
- Boxing Day Brands, Scott-Brown, second
- Later owned by John Woolfe and Gordon Lee who raced with success
- Advertised extensively by Performance Cars Limited, Brentford, Middlesex, in *Motor Sport* between September 1956 and June 1957
- Advertised in *Motor Sport* December 1969 and in *Road and Track* March 1970 by Brian Classic, Didsbury, Manchester
- Mid 1970 raced by David Duffy
- Advertised for sale by Rod Leach
- Later owned by Peter Hall, UK
- 1994, auctioned by Brooks, sold to Aba Kogan, Canada

XKC 049 fitted with an XK120 windscreen, owned and driven by Gillie Tyrer, approximately 1955
Photo ©JDHT

Joe Kelly in XKC 050 leading Bob Berry in the lightweight XK120 in the Empire Trophy race at Oulton Park in 1955; later in the race Kelly crashed
Photo ©JDHT

XKC 050

Chassis number	XKC 050
Distributor	Caveys, Dublin, Eire
Current owner	Steve Earle, USA
Engine number	E-1049-8
Registration mark	ZU 2357
Axle ratio	3.92
Body number	K-1050
Date of dispatch	18 August 1953
Colour, original	British Racing Green
Colour, current interior trim	British Racing Green with Green

XKC 050 history:

- Last production car built
- Sold to Joe Kelly
- 5 September 1953, Tourist Trophy, Dundrod, with Jack Fairman, second in class, seventh overall
- 11 September 1953,Wakefield Trophy, The Curragh, second
- 12 September 1953, O'Boyle Trophy Handicap, The Curragh, fifth
- 10 July 1954, Leinster Trophy, Wicklow, second
- 28 August 1954, Wakefield Trophy, The Curragh, second
- 29 August 1954, O'Boyle Handicap, The Curragh, third
- 1954, Dundrod Tourist Trophy, lent to Joe Flynn and Torrie Large, fifth in class, thirteenth overall
- 9 July 1955, Empire Trophy, Oulton Park, crashed
- Later owners included Paul Emery, C Unsworth
- 1959 - 1960, Keith Jeans, Dorset, registered 333 GMT
- David Harvey, Surrey, sold in 1965
- Jeremy Broad, Warwickshire
- Bryan Corser, Shrewsbury, registered SVM 737, two year rebuild, owned until 1980
- D K Engineering advertised car for sale 1983
- 1983-84, Robert Baker, Omaha, USA,
- 1984, sold to Steve Earle, USA, registered HV 6228
- 9 June 1985, Kansas City Grand Prix, David Love driving, fifth
- 4 August 1985, St Louis Grand Prix, Steve Earle, third
- 25 August 1985, Monterey Historic race, driven by Tony Swan, fourth
- 1986, Mille Miglia, Steve Earle
- 1987, Mille Miglia, Steve Earle
- 24 August 1987, Monterey Historic race, Murray Smith, first
- 1989, Mille Miglia, Steve Earle
- August 1989, Monterey Historic race, Larry Crane, fifth
- August 1991, Monterey Historic race, Murray Smith, fifteenth
- August 1992, Monterey Historic race, Murray Smith, sixth
- August 1993, Monterey Historic race, Murray Smith, fourth
- August 1994, Monterey Historic race, Murray Smith, fourth
- October 1997, Coronado Speed Festival, John Anderson, first
- August 1998, Monterey Historic race, John Anderson, fifth
- October 1998, Coronado Speed Festival, John Anderson, second
- May 1999, Wine Country Classic, John Anderson, first
- September 1999, Goodwood Revival Meeting, Steve Earle
- May 2000, Monaco Historique Grand Prix, Steve Earle
- 19 August 2000, Monterey Historic race, Justin Law first

XKC 051

Chassis number	XKC 051
Distributor	n/a
Current owner	Adrian Hamilton, UK
Engine number	E-1053-8
Registration mark	LSF 420 (original)
Axle ratio	n/a
Body number	n/a
Date of dispatch	n/a
Colour, original	British Racing Green
Colour, current	British Racing Green with Green interior trim

Duncan Hamilton in XKC 051, the winning car, at Mulsanne corner during the 1953 Le Mans
Photo ©JDHT

XKC 051 works car history:

- Works 'lightweight', 1953 Le Mans, Rolt/Hamilton (Dunlop disc brakes, Weber carburettors, cylinder head number RJ 65, 2.93:1 axle, race number 18), first
- 1953, Tourist Trophy, Rolt/Hamilton (9.1 compression, 3.54:1 axle, race number 6), retired
- 1953, Prescott, Walker (4.27:1 axle), fastest sports car of the day
- 1954, sold to Ecurie Ecosse, painted Metallic Blue
- Also, car bearing number 18 put on show at Ford Motor Company's '40 Years of Sports Cars' exhibition at Detroit Museum in January/February 1954
- British Empire Trophy, Oulton Park, Rolt third in heat, Sanderson fifth in handicap final and second on road
- First Easter Handicap, Goodwood, Rolt, second
- Members' Meeting, Goodwood, race two, Sanderson, third after spinning when in second place; race four, Sanderson crashed
- *Daily Express* International Sports Car Race, Silverstone, Peter Walker, third and team prize
- Aintree, Scott-Douglas, sixth
- Snetterton, Scott-Douglas, fourth, eighth, and retired
- Goodwood, Scott-Douglas, twelfth and thirteenth
- Oulton Park, Titterington first and Scott-Douglas, second
- Charterhall, Lawrence, first
- Silverstone Grand Prix Meeting, Titterington, sixth
- Zandvoort, Scott-Douglas, second
- 1955, British Empire Trophy, Oulton Park, Sanderson, sixth in class and sixteenth on handicap
- Easter Goodwood, Rolt, fourth
- Car was sold to Bill Smith, colour changed to red
- Ulster Trophy race, Dundrod, first
- Eastern Counties 100, Snetterton, third
- Sold to Geoffrey Allison
- 1956, colour changed to white and used for successful club racing season
- Mallory Park, first
- Sold to Miles Brubacher, USA and used as road car in 1957
- 1968, chassis restored
- Sold to Briggs Cunningham and displayed at Costa Mesa Museum, California
- Sold to Adrian Hamilton
- Rebuilt by David Cottingham and re-bodied by RS Panels in 14 swg, colour British Racing Green
- Original 18 swg body retained by Hamilton but not used due to poor condition and impracticality
- 1991 and 1993 Jaguar factory cavalcade to Le Mans
- Still owned by Adrian Hamilton, UK, and is the only 'works' Le Mans winning Jaguar in existence. The 1951 and 1955 winners were both broken up, and the 1956 and 1957 D-types were entered by Ecurie Ecosse.

The classic study of Hamilton leaving the pit in XKC 051 during the 1953 Le Mans
Photo ©JDHT

Two of the works cars, XKC 053 with the winner XKC 051 behind, at Le Mans in 1953
Photo ©JDHT

The Jaguar works team prior to the start of the 1953 Le Mans race - the cars are XKC 053, 051 and 052 (from left to right)
Photo ©JDHT

Hamilton (driving), Rolt (in sunglasses) and mechanics on the lap of honour after winning the 1953 Le Mans
Photo ©JDHT

Rolt in the XKC 051 during the 1953 Le Mans
Photo ©JDHT

XKC 052

Chassis number	XKC 052
Distributor	n/a
Current owner	Privately owned, USA
Engine number	E-1054-8
Registration mark	LFS 672 (original)
Axle ratio	n/a
Body number	n/a
Date of dispatch	8 December 1953
Colour, original	British Racing Green
Colour, current	Metallic Blue

XKC 052, driven by Peter Whitehead, 1953 Le Mans, finished fourth
Photo Klemantaski/JDHT

XKC 052 works car history:

- Works 'lightweight', 1953 Le Mans, Whitehead/Stewart, fourth (Dunlop disc brakes, Weber carburettors, cylinder head number RJ 78, 3.31:1 axle, race number 19)
- Silverstone, Rolt (with engine number E1058-8, cylinder head number RJ 47, 4.09:1 axle), retired
- Goodwood 9 Hours, Rolt/Hamilton (with engine number E1052-9, 3.92:1 axle, race number 2), retired
- 12 February 1953, tested by Norman Dewis in preparation for sale to Ecurie Ecosse
- 1954, sold to Ecurie Ecosse (with engine number E1055-9, 3.31:1 axle), painted Metallic Blue
- 1954, Argentine 1000 kms, Ian Stewart/Jimmy Stewart, crashed
- Rebuilt at factory
- Henceforth Jimmy Stewart during 1954 unless stated otherwise
- British Empire Trophy, Oulton Park, fourth in heat, sixth in final
- Easter Handicap, Goodwood, first
- Members' Meeting, Goodwood, race two, first; race four, first
- Ibsley, second to Flockhart in BRM Mark II; race seven, first
- *Daily Express* International Sports Car Race, Silverstone, fourth and team prize
- Aintree, third Snetterton; Roy Salvadori, first place twice, and third
- Whit Sunday Goodwood, first and seventh
- Oulton Park, Sanderson, second and third
- Charterhall, Sanderson, second and third
- Silverstone Grand Prix Meeting, Rolt, tenth
- Zandvoort, Hans Davids, seventh in heat and unplaced in final
- Charterhall, Salvadori, first
- Goodwood, Titterington, fourth
- Barcelona Cup, Salvadori second
- 1955, sold to Peter Blond
- 1955, used for club racing in UK
- Spa, lent to Hans Davids, fourth
- 1956, Maurice Charles, Six Hour handicap race, Silverstone
- 1957, Alan Ensoll who competed successfully in races at Charterhall, Catterick Camp, Rufforth, Full Sutton and Croft. Also hill climbs at Barbon and Catterick, took part in rallies, and even an autocross in Yorkshire!
- 1958, Tom Candlish. Many competitive outings including:
- 28 September, Charterhall, Unlimited Sportscars, fourth
- December, Brands Hatch Formula Libre race, sixth place twice
- 4 July 1959, Rest and be Thankful Hill Climb Championship, first, Unlimited Sportscars
- 5 July, Charterhall, first, Unlimited GT Race
- 12 July, Brands Hatch, BRSCC Formula Libre race.
- 1959, Ian Denny
- 1969, Brian Classic
- 1970, Paul Grist
- 1971, Martin Morris
- 1991 and 1993, Jaguar factory cavalcades to Le Mans
- 2000, looked after by Miles Morris (Martin's son), and restored between 1986 and 1988
- 2000, sold and now in private ownership in USA

England supervising Hamilton in XKC 052 during the nine hour race at Goodwood, 1953
Photo ©JDHT

XKC 053

Chassis number	XKC 053
Distributor	n/a
Current owner	Privately owned, USA
Engine number	E-1055-8
Registration mark	WKA 9
Axle ratio	n/a
Body number	n/a
Date of dispatch	8 December 1953
Colour, original	British Racing Green
Colour, current	British Racing Green with Green interior trim

XKC 053 works car history:

- Works 'lightweight', 1953 Le Mans, Moss/Walker (Dunlop disc brakes, Weber carburettors, cylinder head number RJ 35, 2.93:1 axle, race number 17), second
- Lisbon Grand Prix, Moss (with engine number 1055-8, 3.31:1 axle) second
- Goodwood Nine Hours, Whitehead/Stewart (with engine number 1055-8, 3.92:1 axle race number 3), third
- Tourist Trophy, Moss/Walker (with engine number 1054-9, 3.54:1 axle, race number 7), retired but lap record to Walker
- 25 November 1953, tested by Norman Dewis in preparation for Ecurie Ecosse
- Sold to Ecurie Ecosse (with engine number E1051-9, 3.31:1 axle), painted Metallic Blue and registered LSF 671
- Argentine 1000 kms, Sanderson/Scott-Douglas (race number 22), fourth
- Castle Combe, Jimmy Stewart, second
- British Empire Trophy, Oulton Park, Sanderson, second in heat, not used in final due to damaged oil cooler
- Ibsley, Sanderson, second and third
- Silverstone, Sanderson, team prize
- Aintree, Sanderson, fifth
- Snetterton, Titterington, third, and two fourth places
- Goodwood, Sanderson, second and eighth
- Oulton Park, Sanderson, broke valve in practice
- Silverstone Grand Prix Meeting, Sanderson, eighth
- Zandvoort, Sanderson, second in heat and first in final
- The Curragh, Titterington, retired
- Charterhall, Sanderson second
- Barcelona Cup, Sanderson, third
- Sold to J K Hunter
- 1955, raced by John Lawrence
- 1956, sold to Gillie Tyrer, reregistered WKA 9 and used for club racing
- Owned by Rupert Ropner
- Owned for many years by Tom Gibson, UK
- Restored by owner and David Hodgson
- Early 1960s raced by Keith Schellenberg
- Converted by Dick Protheroe to 3.8 litres
- Church Fenton, covered standing quarter mile in 12.6 seconds
- 1988, sold, via Adrian Hamilton to Alan Lawson, UK
- 1991, Jaguar factory cavalcade to Le Mans
- 1992, sold to Bob Baker, USA
- 1993, Jaguar factory cavalcade to Le Mans
- 1995, mechanically rebuilt and prepared for historic racing by Terry Larson
- 1996, sold to Kerry Manolas, Australia
- 1998, sold, and now in private ownership in the USA

Moss in XKC 053 is about to pass the Ferrari of Ascari and Villoresi during the 1953 Le Mans
Photo ©JDHT

XKC 054

This car was not really a C-type but should still be mentioned. It was built in 1953 and the entry in the record book simply states that it had a 'special light alloy box frame chassis' and was allocated to the experimental department. According to Andrew Whyte, the car was photographed as early as May 1953 and was fitted with engine number E-1054-9. The body resembled the D-type more than a C-type. Norman Dewis tested this car in Belgium in October 1953 at up to 180mph, and it was still being tested at Le Mans in the spring of 1954, but then disappeared from sight. It is known to have been broken up at the Jaguar factory.

Norman Dewis at Jabbeke in Belgium, speed testing XKC 054 in October 1953
Photo ©JDHT

Peter Whitehead during tyre tests with XKC 054, Reims, spring 1954
Photo ©JDHT

Appendix: Glossary of terms

Definitions related to authenticity, continuous history and transformations, abridged version of the brilliant text created by the late Denis Jenkinson many years ago.

Original:	Does not really exist, as it calls for an unused car in perpetual storage, with all components as fitted by the factory...
Genuine:	All major components must be original, while minor items might be identical substitutes, renewed due to normal wear.
Authentic:	All repairs have been made with original type spares (reproductions allowed for minor items).
Resurrection:	Entity lost, copy created using several major components originating from one car only.
Reconstruction:	Resurrection, which has been based on one major component only, plus collection of items from other cars.
Facsimile:	Copy car built by original manufacturers, many years after initial production ceased.
Duplicate:	Reconstruction, based on 'assorted box of random bits'.
Replica:	Copy, possibly with differences under the skin.
Fake:	By-product of greed, where the result of a Reconstruction or a Duplicate gradually takes on the identity of an Original, Genuine, or Authentic car, possibly after passing through several owners. The present keeper might in good faith be absolutely convinced that he owns a genuine article...
Transformation:	Car with continuous history and changes in form, appearance or structure.

Unbroken and Continuous History means simply that the car involved has been a known car with a complete chain of ownership. This is very important.

Regarding the term 'Genuine', it is a generally accepted rule among recognised experts that, 'a car does not achieve its final identity until it has left the factory for the last time.' One example of this would be if a car returned to the factory for an engine replacement - this engine would now be considered genuine for the car. Also, if a car was crashed and returned to the factory for rebuild, whatever components the factory chose to use in the rebuilding of the car would now be genuine. A final example would be the XKSS. These were all originally built as D-types, and were later converted to XKSS specification by the Jaguar factory.

Concerning the expression 'Transformations', a car may retain impeccable Provenance despite major 'Technical Transformation' (consisting of change of some - or even all - components to identical items of the same specification), provided that the car in question has unbroken and continuous history. 'Transformation' can also be used to describe a car with unbroken history, but combined with major changes in specification (such as a different type of chassis frame, suspension, engine, transmission, brakes etc.).

Bibliography

Journals:

Autosport
Jaguar Journal
Jaguar Quarterly
Motor Sport
News and Technical Bulletin (Classic Jaguar Association)
Road and Track
The Autocar
The Motor

Published papers:

Berry, Robert 'Motor Racing and the Manufacturer', a paper read to the San Francisco branch of the American Society of Automotive Engineers, August 1976, subsequently published by British Leyland Inc., Leonia, NJ, USA

Heynes, William 'The Jaguar Engine', a paper read to the Institution of Mechanical Engineers (Automobile Division) in London on 14 April 1953, subsequently reprinted in *The Motor*, 15 and 22 April 1953, and *The Autocar*, 24 April 1953

Skilleter, Paul 'The C-type Jaguar – Specification and world listing', in *Jaguar Quarterly*, vol.4 no.2, November/December 1991

Books:

Clausager, Anders Ditlev *Jaguar – A Living Legend* (Brian Trodd, London, 1990)

Clausager, Anders Ditlev *Le Mans* (Arthur Barker, London, 1982)

Hodges, David *The Le Mans 24-Hour Race* (Temple Press, London, 1963)

Levy, Burt *The Last Open Road* (Think Fast Ink, Oak Park, Illinois, USA, 1994)

Montagu of Beaulieu with Sedgwick, Michael *Jaguar – A Biography* (Batsford, London, 1961, and later editions)

Porter, Philip *Jaguar Sports Racing Cars* (Bay View Books, Bideford, 1995)

Skilleter, Paul *Jaguar Sports Cars* (Haynes, Sparkford, 1975 and later editions; revised edition forthcoming)

Skilleter, Paul *Jaguar – The Sporting Heritage* (Virgin, London, 2000)

Whyte, Andrew Jaguar – *The History of a Great British Car* (Patrick Stephens, Cambridge, 1980 and later editions; revised edition forthcoming)

Whyte, Andrew *Jaguar Sports Racing and Works Competition Cars to 1953* (Haynes, Sparkford, 1982; revised edition forthcoming)